Managing and Improving Your Cash Flow

Managing and Improving Your Cash Flow

Dr. Jae K. Shim, MBA, Ph.D.

Professor of Accounting and Finance
California State University, Long Beach
and
CEO, Delta Consulting Company

GLOBAL
professional
publishing

Global Professional Publishing Ltd
Random Acres
Slip Mill Lane
Hawkhurst
Cranbrook
Kent TN18 5AD
Email: publishing@gppbooks.com

ISBN 978-1-906403-63-8

Printed by Berforts, United Kingdom

Contents

Preface

Profit and cash flow – they are often confused but very, very different. This book will teach to distinguish between them and gives you the tools and techniques that will allow you to both effectively increase your cash flow and manage your it efficiently. *Manage and Improve Your Cash Flow* covers all aspects of cash management and decisions, ranging from cash flow forecasting and budgeting, to internal control of cash, and to short-term financing. A variety of tools you will need to manage, and understand, cash inflows and outflows are explained and illustrated, including banking relationships, collection and payment management systems, cash flow management software, and optimal cash balance.

This book is unique in three special ways. First, the book is practically oriented. It avoids theoretical, rigorous, and mathematical discussions, giving you just enough information to understand how to use them. It will directly get into how to use any particular method or tool, when to use it, what it can be used for, and what resources are required of it. Finally *Manage and Improve Your Cash Flow* includes a great many practical examples, applications, illustrations, guidelines, measures, checklists, rules of thumb, tips, graphs, diagrams, and tables to aid your comprehension of the subject.

All in all, after studying this book you will truly be able to manage and improve your cash flow effectively and efficiently.

Dr. Jae K. Shim

Dr. Jae K. Shim is one of the most prolific accounting and finance experts in the world. He is a professor of accounting and finance at California State University, Long Beach and CEO of Delta Consulting Company, a financial consulting and training firm. Dr. Shim received his M.B.A. and Ph.D. degrees from the University of California at Berkeley (Haas School of Business). He has been a consultant to commercial and nonprofit organizations for over 30 years.

Dr. Shim has over 50 college and professional books to his credit, including, *Barron's Accounting Handbook, Barron's Dictionary of Accounting Terms, 2011 GAAP: Handbook of Policies and Procedures, Budgeting Basics and Beyond, 2010-2011 Corporate Controller's Handbook of Financial Management, US Master Finance Guide, Uses and Analysis of Financial Statements, Investment Sourcebook, Dictionary of Real Estate, Dictionary of International Investment Terms, Dictionary of Business Terms, The Vest-Pocket CPA, The Vest-Pocket CFO,* and the best-selling *Vest-Pocket MBA*.

Thirty of his publications have been translated into foreign languages such as Chinese, Spanish, Russian, Polish, Croatian, Italian, Japanese, and Korean. Professor Shim's books have been published by CCH, Barron's, John Wiley, McGraw-Hill, Prentice-Hall, Penguins Portfolio, Thomson Reuters, Global Professional Publishing, American Management Association (Amacom), and the American Institute of CPAs (AICPA).

Dr. Shim has also published numerous articles in professional and academic journals. He was the recipient of the Financial Management Association International's *1982 Credit Research Foundation Award* for his article on cash flow forecasting and financial modeling.

Dr. Shim has been frequently quoted by such media as the *Los Angeles Times, Orange County Register, Business Start-ups, Personal Finance, and Money Radio.* He also provides business content He also provides business content for CPE e-learning providers and for m-learning providers such as iPhone, iPad, iPod, Blackberry, Android, Droid, and Nokia.

Email: drjaekshim@gmail.com, jaeshim@csulb.edu

Web: www.csulb.edu/~jaeshim

MODULE 1

The Nuts and Bolts

INTRODUCTION

Cash is the Lifeblood of a Business

Cash—-not accounting profits—is king. Cash flows are received by the firm and can be reinvested. Accounting profit—often referred to as the bottom line—is shown on the profit and loss statement when they are earned (accrued) rather than when the money is actually in hand. A firm's cash flows and accounting profits may not occur together.

Sound cash management is the key to the survival of any business. You can go broke even while making a substantial profit. This book alerts you to the difference between accounting profits and cash flows and teaches you the tools and techniques that allow you to effectively increase and manage your cash flow. It is designed for business owners, entrepreneurs, and companies who want to manage their cash in the best possible way. Cash in the sense used in this book is the medium of exchange and refers to how much money the business has on hand and how much is in demand deposits such as savings accounts, checking accounts, and money market accounts. Cash is the money that flows through your business from cash register to bank account to suppliers. You have to put your money to work for you productively!

Without monitoring your cash—measuring it, investing it, borrowing it, and collecting it—you can cheat yourself out of extra profits and end up in trouble with creditors and even in bankruptcy.

Some of the techniques we will discuss include monitoring daily cash positions, timing receipts and payments, analyzing the adequacy of cash balances, budgeting, forecasting cash needs, measuring your ability to pay bills and debts, and dealing with your banker and your bank accounts. Other important points we will explore are how to tell the difference between net income and cash available and what equipment to buy and when to buy it.

Keeping track of your company's cash position is essential, because cash flow is the lifeblood of a small business and is fundamental to its existence. Without proper cash flow, you cannot pay your bills on time, which may hurt your business's credit standing. Remember, too, that bankruptcies are caused by lack of cash rather than lack of profit.

Having "enough" cash means having enough available *at the right time*. Poor cash flow can mean the loss of attractive opportunities such as the chance to buy inventory at bargain prices or to pay vendors early in exchange for discounts.

Finally, cash flow is truly a flow, like the tide. Being aware of the different factors that affect this flow is important. Here is a list of some of the factors that contribute to the crests and troughs of cash flow:

- Non-regular disbursement items such as debt repayment, equipment purchases, and store furnishings.
- Seasonal sales that cause fluctuations in cash receipts and cash payments.
- Variations in bi-weekly payrolls; some months have three, while others have only two.
- The placing of large orders in order to obtain volume discounts.
- The payment of sales commissions or bonuses at the end of the year.
- Closing the business for vacations or repairs.

Cash crunch warning signs

Is a cash crunch ahead? Look out for these potential warning signs:

- Cash on hand has been declining for several months
- Receivables are taking longer to collect
- Payables are increasing
- You're putting aside bills that you typically pay on time
- You're unable to pay yourself a regular salary
- You're getting calls from vendors asking about invoice payments
- Your inventory levels are increasing
- You overdraw your checking account expecting new sales to cover it
- You loan the business personal funds to meet routine expenses

Strategies to stave off cash flow crunches

Maintaining healthy cash flow is crucial to your long-term success, yet cash crunches are a perennial problem for many businesses. Even the most successful businesses can have cash flow issues—for example, rapid growth can stress cash flow with the added costs of new employees, expanded inventories, or more equipment. To stave off a potential cash crunch and its adverse consequences follow these essential guidelines.

Keep a close eye on your books

Too many business owners take a quick look at their books and pronounce their finances fit without truly understanding their cash flow situation. While an increase in sales or a solid bank balance may put you at ease, neither one necessarily translates into healthy cash flow. Take time each month to prepare and review financial reports — especially a cash flow statement that specifically details the funds moving in and out of your business. Many accounting software programs (such as QuickBooks or Peachtree) can create these reports for you. Speak with your accountant or financial advisor to learn more about what to look for in these reports.

Pay bills intelligently

One good way to conserve your cash is to make the most of vendor payment terms, which are essentially interest-free loans from your suppliers. Take the maximum amount of time allotted (often 30 or 60 days) to pay invoices — for example, if an invoice is due on the 15th of the month, don't pay it on the 1st. Many businesses now use electronic bill payment solutions, which let them set the exact date a bill is paid and money is withdrawn from their accounts. Talk with your bank to find out if this option is available to you.

Take advantage of incentives

The only time you should pay a bill early is if you get a discount. Some suppliers may offer an incentive for paying their bills quickly, typically within a week or two. It may be worth taking them up on the offer. Think of it this way — a 2% discount on a 30-day invoice translates into a 24% annual return if the money was invested. If your vendors don't offer this, ask for it — they may be willing to do so to speed up their own cash flow.

Organize your receivables schedule

Slow-paying customers are the root of many cash flow problems. Don't let invoices lag. Put yourself on an invoice tracking schedule using your accounting software. Not only can these programs generate invoices, but they can automatically classify accounts receivable by age — e.g. less than 30 days old, between 30 and 60 days, between 60 and 90 days, etc. Review your accounts receivables aging reports frequently so you can take timely action on overdue invoices.

Control your inventory

Money tied up in inventory can dramatically impact cash flow. Retailers and manufacturers are especially vulnerable in this area. Retailers should regularly gauge their inventory turnover ratio (cost of goods sold divided by the average value of inventory) to make sure it is within industry norms. Old or outdated stock should be cleared out through end-of-season sales to turn stale assets into liquid ones. Manufacturers can use supply-chain management tactics to have just enough inventory on hand to keep product lines running and meet customer commitments without tying up critical cash.

Check your prices

Make sure your prices keep pace with rising costs. Many small businesses hesitate to increase their rates because they're afraid they'll lose customers. Customers actually expect their suppliers to institute small, regular price hikes. Also, check your competition regularly — if they're charging higher prices, maybe you should, too.

Consider leasing

Over the long run, leasing costs more than purchasing, but its cash flow benefits can still make it a prudent choice. Leasing computers, cars, and the like lets you avoid tying up cash or lines of credit that might better be used for running your day-to-day business. Lease payments are also considered a business expense, so the tax benefits are maintained even though the items are not purchased.

Always get the best deal

One of the biggest cash drains is spending money needlessly. Avoid this by comparison-shopping for products where service and other value-addons are not critical. Buy in bulk to get price breaks for goods you regularly use in your business. Get quotes from competing suppliers for capital equipment. In addition, check deliveries against invoices to be sure you're getting what you ordered and that you're being charged the correct price.

Healthy cash flow is really about making every dollar count. Make the time and effort to manage your cash flow effectively, and you'll be on the way to long-term profitability.

1 Why is Cash Flow Important?

Businesses need an adequate cash flow to support customer balances, purchase merchandise for resale, meet operating expenses, and pay debt. As a rule of thumb, a retailer should have a *monthly net cash flow* (cash receipts less cash payments) of at least three times the amount of customer balances. A sufficient cash balance is required for normal business operations, since inventory must be paid for before the business receives any cash from sales of that inventory to customers. The longer the time period from cash payment for inventory to cash receipts from sales, the higher the cash balance should be; a declining trend in the cash balance may portend a looming "cash crisis."

Business owners need to manage what they owe and to make sure they do not get in debt too deeply. There is nothing worse than having to tell a lender, creditor, or the Internal Revenue Service that you cannot pay. Owners should analyze their payment schedule to ensure that it is reasonable and keep accurate records of how much money they owe, and for how long, to avoid being assessed interest penalties for excessive delays in payment.

One way to save on cash is to cut excessive costs such as wages, travel, and entertainment. You may also discontinue the manufacture of products that are losing money and avoid buying assets that require huge cash outlays and yet have long and uncertain payback periods.

2 Cash Management Objectives and Decisions

Plan, manage, monitor, and control cash flows in order to create an acceptable balance between holding too little and too much cash. The ideal cash management system allows the small business to operate for extended periods with cash balances near or at a level of zero. It is possible only under two conditions: (1) a perfect forecast of future net cash flows (cash inflows *minus* cash outflows) and (2) perfect matching of cash receipts and disbursements. Unfortunately, these two conditions are not commonly found. *Note:* Perfect cash forecasting is not possible; inflows and outflows do not occur at the same time in the same amounts. Some inflows and outflows are uncertain, others are irregular, and still others are continual.

Some of the objectives of cash management are:

- To reduce the need to borrow and, if necessary, to borrow at lower interest costs.
- To minimize idle cash balances.
- To maximize the return on surplus funds.
- To reduce bank charges and keep transaction costs as low as possible.

Your cash management decisions must take into account your answers to the following questions:

- What can be done to speed up collections and stretch out cash outflows'?
- How can I stabilize cash flows? For example, can I add a non-seasonal product to my seasonal products?

- How can I earn the best return on my money?
- When should I arrange for financing, and how much do I need? How are my cash flows affected during periods of inflation and recession?
- How much of a cash balance should I hold at different times during the year? This is especially important for a seasonal business.
- Where should I invest my excess cash and for what time period (e.g., 3-month treasury bill, 6-month certificate of deposit)?
- Are any of my cash balances restricted and so unavailable for use? For example a compensating balance at the bank is funds held as collateral for a loan.

3 Key Cash Management Considerations

In making cash decisions, always take into account not only the current period but future periods. Cash decisions have to consider all the factors and interrelationships that affect cash flow.

Simply put, get the best use out of your cash by *receiving* cash sooner and *paying* cash later. Other important considerations include:

- Where is the cash inflow coming from and how dependable is it?
- What are your cash payment demands? If you do not watch your cash, you may experience financial difficulties; for example, a rapidly growing small business may run out of money. *Note:* Paying dividends without proper cash budgeting is not a good option unless the company has a strategic reason to make shareholders satisfied.

What determines how much cash you should hold? The key factors are:

- Cash management policies
- Current funds position
- Rate of return
- Risk levels
- Loan payment schedules and maturity dates
- Your ability to borrow or use credit wisely
- Expected short- and long-term cash flow
- Economic conditions
- The probabilities of receiving cash or paying it under different scenarios; for example, is your cash protected to guard against loss?

As a rule, your cash management goal should be to invest cash to earn interest while still having enough funds on hand to pay bills. You need to be *liquid*, meaning that you have the ability to convert your assets (what you own) into cash without significant loss of value, so you can pay your current debts and meet unexpected demands and contingencies. This requires planning about when surplus funds can be invested and when you must borrow.

If you have several bank accounts, you may be able to guard against accumulating excessive balances. One way of doing this is to establish a *line of credit* (LOC) that allows you to borrow immediately up to a predetermined dollar amount. (For more on LOCs, see below). Such an agreement often lets you keep a lower cash balance than you would otherwise need.

If your business is financially strong, you may be able to borrow at favorable interest rates without loan restrictions. The financial soundness of your business depends on many factors, including its debt position and stability in sales.

You may find that your cash is tied up unproductively, for instance in excess inventory, receivables, and advances to employees. Furthermore, the cash in some bank accounts may be restricted. A bank, for example, may require a deposit of funds as collateral to guarantee a loan. This restricted deposit is referred to as a *compensating balance*. Unfortunately, you do not earn interest on this balance.

You may also use a savings account as security for a loan. In this case, your funds are on hold until the loan is repaid.

Another factor to look at is whether banking services are cost-effective. Analyse each bank account as to (1) type, (2) balance, and (3) cost. What are the bank charges and are the services paid for, such as the processing cost for checks, worth it?

Lock in a line of credit

One of the most effective tools a business can use to survive a cash crunch is a line of credit (LOC), a revolving financing tool that you can tap into on an as-needed basis. With a LOC, your lender sets a maximum amount of funds it will make available to you; you can access those funds when your business needs them. Typically, interest accrues only when you use the funds, and is charged only on the outstanding balance. The borrower has the option of paying back the balance in full or over time. When you repay the principal, money is made available for future loans.

LOCs are especially well suited to short-tem cash flow issues, allowing you to cover any shortfalls between anticipated revenues and expenses. They are also valuable for seasonal businesses where purchases need to be made in advance of incoming sales.

Be aware that the best time to get a credit line is when you don't need it If you're in the midst of a cash crunch, it's likely a lender will deem you too high a risk and turn your application down. Instead, approach lenders when your finances are in good shape to improve your chances of being approved. To learn more about LOCs, speak with your banker or other financial services provider.

MODULE 2

Analysis of Cash Flow

4 The Difference between Cash Flow and Earnings

Cash flow is quite different from earnings (profit, net income) reported on the income statement. Earnings is an accounting concept created by accounting convention, while cash flow is based on the timing of the receipts and disbursements of cash. Under the *accrual basis*, revenue is recognized when earned and expenses are recognized when incurred; net income equals revenue less expenses. Net income measured on the accrual basis does not reflect the receipt or payment of cash. On the other hand, under the cash basis of accounting, revenue is recognized only when cash is actually received and expenses are recorded only when cash is actually paid; the difference between cash revenue and cash expense is cash earnings.

A small business moves on *cash* rather than profits. You must have cash, not net income, to pay bills or loans; you have to pay workers money, not earnings. A small business needs cash to finance growth and to provide stability in downward markets. Even if the business has high profits, it does not necessarily mean it is generating cash flow from operations; net income must be converted to cash earnings when considering the cash flow from operations of the business

The following items make earnings and cash two entirely different concepts:

Sales/accounts receivable

Sales made on credit represent revenue that increases your profit; however, cash flow is affected only when the receivable is collected! *Don't forget*: Money is tied up in accounts receivable. (See Keys 28 and 29 for more on accounts receivable.)

Inventory

The accountant's matching concept requires that inventory be charged to cost of sales (which reduces earnings) when a sale takes place. *Don't forget*: Money is tied up in inventory of raw materials, work-in-process (partially completed goods on the assembly line), and finished goods (completed goods available for sale).

Noncash charges

Noncash charges such as depreciation and amortization are deducted from sales revenue to arrive at earnings, but they do not involve cash outlays. They are periodic charges created by accounting convention.

Prepaid items

Prepaid items such as insurance, rents, and service contracts are cash payments made in advance. They reduce earnings in future periods, not in the period of payment.

Fixed assets

Fixed assets such as property, plant, and equipment reduce cash by both the initial down payment and all subsequent installments. Earnings, on the other hand, are affected only by depreciation (the yearly decline in value of a fixed asset arising from wear and tear, natural deterioration, and obsolescence). Land is an exception since it is not depreciable.

Constant payments on interest-bearing obligations

Most interest-bearing obligations require monthly payments of principal and interest until the obligation is fully paid. Only the interest portion of the payment is reflected in earnings, whereas cash flow is affected by *both* principal and interest.

Example

The following example illustrates the difference between the cash basis and accrual basis.

Sarah Cohen started a consulting practice on January 1. For the month of January, she rendered professional services and billed out $5,000. These bills were not paid until February. She also received $2,500 in January for other services. During January, she incurred expenses of $1,500 but paid out only $1,250. Based on this information, her cash earnings for January were $1,250 but her net income was $6,000 as shown below.

January 20x11

	CASH BASIS	ACCRUAL BASIS
Fee income	$2,500	$7,500
Less: Expenses	1,250	1,500
Cash earnings	$1,250	
Net income		6,000

As an example, assume a small business owner wants to determine his or her cash earnings (cash flow from operations) based on the following income statement data: net income $170,000, depreciation expense $5,000, and amortization expense $2,000. The cash earnings are $177,000, as computed below:

Net income	$170,000
Add: Noncash expenses	
Depreciation	5,000
Amortization	2,000
	$177,000

5 How to Go Broke While Making a Profit

If you are to manage cash flows, you must understand (1) the difference between the profits you see on the bottom line of the income statement and economic profits, and (2) how accounting profits differ from economic profits, which is *cash flows*.

The following example illustrates an important point you should know about: You can go broke even while showing accounting profits!

As the year started, Mr. Parker of the Office Products Company was in fine shape. His company made ballpoint pens for 75 cents each and sold them for $1. He kept a 30-day supply in inventory, paid his bills promptly, and billed his customers 30 days net. Sales were right on target, with the sales manager predicting a steady increase. It felt like his lucky year, and it began this way.

Office Products Company
Balance Sheet
January 1, 2x11

Cash	$1,000	Liabilities	0
Inventory	750		
Receivables	1,000	Retained Earnings	$2,750
Total Assets	2,750	Total Liabilities & Equity	$2,750

In January, he sold 1,000 ballpoint pens, shipped them at a cost of $750, collected his receivables- winding up with a tidy $250 profit- and his books looked like this:

January 31, 2x11

Cash	$1,250	Liabilities	0	
Inventory	750			
Receivables	1,000	Retained Earnings	$3,000	($2,750 + $250)
Total Assets	$3,000	Total Liabilities & Equity	$3,000	

February's sales jumped to 1,500 ballpoint pens. With a corresponding step-up in production to maintain his 30-day inventory, he made 2,000 pens at a cost of $1,500. All receivables from January were collected. The profit so far is: $625 ($250 + $375). Now his books looked like this:

February 28, 2x11

Cash	$750	Liabilities	0	
Inventory	1,125			
Receivables	1,500	Retained earnings	$3,375	($3,000 + $375)
Total Assets	$3,375	Total Liabilities & Equity	$3,375	

March sales were even better with 2,000 units sold. Collections were also on time. Production, to adhere to his inventory policy, was 2,500 units. Operating results for the month: $500 profit; profit to date: $1,125. His books now show:

March 31, 2x11

Cash	$375	Liabilities	0	
Inventory	1,500			
Receivables	2,000	Retained Earnings	$3,875	($3,375 + $500)
Total Assets	$3,875	Total Liabilities & Equity	$3,875	

In April, sales jumped another 500 units to 2,500—and Parker patted his sales manager on the back. His customers were paying right on time. Production was pushed to 3,000 units, and the month's business netted him $625 for a profit to date of $1,750. He took off to Florida before he saw the accountant's report:

April 30, 2x11

Cash	$125	Liabilities	0	
Inventory	1,875			
Receivables	2,500	Retained Earnings	$4,500	($3,875 + $625)
Total Assets	$4,500	Total Liabilities & Equity	$4,500	

May saw Parker's small business really taking off—sales of 3,000 units, production of 3,500, and a five-month profit of $2,500. But, suddenly, he got a phone call from his bookkeeper: "Come home! We need money!" His books had caught up with him:

May 31, 2x11

Cash	$ 0	Liabilities	0	
Inventory	2,250			
Receivables	3,000	Retained Earnings	$5,250	($4,500 + $750)
Total Assets	$5,250	Total Liabilities & Equity	$5,250	

To capture the critical interactions and relationships between net income and cash flow, the preceding table lists the sources and uses of cash. The message is clear: you can go broke while making a profit. Parker's cash was down to zero, while the business made a five-month profit of $2,500.

In appraising his cash flow from operations, the small business owner must determine which income statement items generate or use cash. For example, even though credit sales increase profit, it does not increase cash until collected.

Office Products Company
Statement of Cash Flows
For the Month Ended June 30, 2x11

	FEB.	MARCH	APRIL	MAY	JUNE	TOTAL
Cash Balance (a)	1,000	1,250	750	375	125	1,000
Sources of Cash						
Profits (b)	$250	$375	$500	$625	$750	$2,500
Uses of Cash						
Inventory	0	500	500	500	500	2,000
Receivables	0	375	375	375	375	1,500
Total (c)	0	875	875	875	875	3,500
Increase (Decrease) (d)	250	($500)	($375)	($250)	($125)	($1,000)
Cash Balance (e)	$1,250	$750	$375	$125	$0	$0

Note: (d) = (b) - (c) and (e) = (a) + (d)

6 How Do You Know if You are Liquid?

Liquidity means you have sufficient cash and are able to meet short-term business debts when due. You need to be liquid to carry out normal daily business operations, especially when things are tough. Without liquidity, meeting expenses and paying creditors will be difficult. As previously mentioned, it is advisable to have a line of credit with the bank to obtain funds when needed. You may also obtain funds by selling some of your short-term investments.

If you are illiquid, you have a serious financial problem. On the other hand, if you have excessive marketable securities, you are earning a lower rate of return than if you hold noncurrent assets (e.g., real estate). Cash is the most liquid asset, but it does not provide a return.

Analyzing business liquidity

You may compute and analyze various financial ratios to determine if your business is liquid. One way to do this is by using the current ratio. The *current ratio* equals current assets divided by current liabilities. It reveals whether you can satisfy current liabilities with current assets. The current ratio typically should be at least two to one, meaning that you should have $2 in current assets for every $1 in current liabilities. If you are likely to have difficulty borrowing funds from the bank to meet unexpected needs, this ratio should be even higher.

Another ratio you can use to determine liquidity is the quick ratio. The *quick ratio* equals cash plus marketable securities plus accounts receivable divided by current liabilities. These assets are the ones that are most "quickly" convertible into cash. Remember, inventory and prepaid expenses are excluded. The quick ratio is a stringent measure of liquidity. It should typically be at least one to one.

Another measure of liquidity is the accounts receivable turnover. The *accounts receivable turnover* equals annual credit sales divided by average accounts receivable.

Average accounts receivable equals beginning plus ending receivables divided by two. The "turnover" indicates how fast you are collecting from customers. Obviously, a faster collection is best, since you know you get your money and can invest it for a return. The *collection period* equals 365 days divided by the accounts receivable turnover. It tells you how many days it takes to collect money owed you.

Are customers paying later than the credit terms you are offering? If so, why, and what can you do about it? For example, if your terms of sale are payable in 60 days and customers are paying on average in 120 days, you have a problem! An "aging schedule" listing how many days each customer's account is outstanding may be prepared.

At the same time, you do not want money tied up in excessive inventory that could be invested elsewhere for a return. There may be substantial costs of storing and insuring the goods, and obsolescence and spoilage risks may exist. Useful ratios in analyzing inventory are the *inventory turnover* (cost of goods sold divided by the average inventory) and *average age of inventory* (365 days divided by the inventory turnover). It is desirable for inventory to turn over quickly so cash is received and inventory holding costs are minimized. The condition of inventory is best when it is recently acquired.

Another important item pertaining to liquidity is the operating cycle, or how long it takes to go from cash to cash. The *operating cycle* is the number of days from cash to inventory to accounts receivable to cash. It equals the collection period plus the age of inventory. A short operating cycle is best.

A retailer provides the following financial information:

	2x12	2x11	2x10
Cash	$30,000	$35,000	
Marketable Securities	20,000	15,000	
Accounts Receivable	20,000	15,000	$10,000
Inventory	50,000	45,000	50,000
Total Current Assets	$120,000	$110,000	
Current Liabilities	55,400	50,000	
Sales	80,000	102,000	
Cost of Goods Sold	50,000	60,000	

The current ratio (current assets/current liabilities) for 2x12 was 2.17 ($120,000/$55,400), and for 2x11 it was 2.2 ($110,000/$50,000). There was a very slight decline in the current ratio, indicating that liquidity remained nearly constant.

The quick ratio (cash + marketable securities + accounts receivable/current liabilities) was 1.26 ($30,000 + $20,000 +$20,000/$55,400) in 2x12. The ratio for 2x11 was 1.3 ($35,000 + $15,000 + $15,000/$50,000). The retailer's stringent liquidity measure was only slightly less, indicating that liquidity remained about the same.

The average accounts receivable (beginning + ending/2) for 2x12 was $17,500 ($20,000 + $15,000/2). The accounts receivable turnover (net credit sales/average accounts receivable) was 4.57 times ($80,000/$17,500); in 2x11, the turnover was 8.16 ($102,000/$12,500). The drop in this ratio in 2x12 is significant and indicates a serious problem in collecting from customers. The retailer in this example needs to reevaluate its credit policy, which may be too lax, or its billing collection policy, or both.

The collection period (365/accounts receivable turnover) for 2x12 was 79.9 days (365/4.57), and for 2x11 it was 44.7 days (365/8.16). This means it took almost 80 days in 2x12 for a sale to be converted into cash. There was a substantial increase in collection days in 2x12, indicating a danger that customer balances may become uncollectible. One possible reason for this increase may be that the retailer is selling to risky customers. The next step would be to question what the retailer's credit terms are and how this compares to the time that receivables are outstanding.

Average inventory (beginning + ending/2) for 2x12 was $47,500 ($50,000 + $45,000/2). Inventory turnover (cost of goods sold/average inventory) for 2x12 was 1.05 times ($50,000/$47,500). In 2x11, the inventory turnover was 1.26 times ($60,000/$47,500). The decline in inventory turnover indicates increased stocking of goods. The retailer should determine whether specific inventory categories are not selling well and, if this is the case, the reasons why; however, a "decline" in the turnover rate would not cause concern if it were primarily due to the introduction of a new product line for which the effects of the retailer's advertising have not yet been felt.

The average age of inventory (365/inventory turnover) for 2x12 was 347.6 days (365/1.05). In 2x11, the age was 289.7 (365/1.26). The lengthening of the holding period shows a greater risk of obsolescence.

The operating cycle equals:

	AVERAGE COLLECTION PERIOD	+	AGE OF INVENTORY	
2x12	79.9 days	+	347.6 days	= 427.5 days
2x11	44.7 days	+	289.7 days	=334.4 days

This is an unfavorable trend, since an increased amount of money is being tied up in noncash assets.

In general, liquidity ratios are designed to identify liquidity problems so you can take appropriate corrective action to ensure that you will be able to meet a cash crisis.

7 Cash Utilization and Adequacy

Cash utilization indicates how well your small business is using its money in running the business, keeping liquid to pay bills and earning a return. Cash availability measures how much money is free to pay your operating expenses and debt payments. Adequate cash flow is needed not only to stay afloat but also for expansion and the purchase of new assets.

The need for cash and its utilization depends upon the type of small business: a retail store selling high-priced appliances needs more cash to buy expensive inventory than a service-oriented business such as an accounting firm having no inventory.

You may want to compute some cash ratios to get a handle on how efficient the utilization and adequacy of your cash balance is.

A high ratio of sales to cash (called *cash turnover*) may reveal a cash shortage that ultimately can result in problems paying bills if you have no other ready source of funds. A low ratio of sales to cash may mean idle cash balances, resulting in a lower return being earned. (However, cash accumulated for specific purposes or contingencies may result in a *temporary* drop in the cash turnover ratio.)

Let's assume you report the following data for your small business:

	2X11	2X12
Cash	$50,000	$40,000
Sales	800,000	900,000

The turnover of cash is 16 ($800,000/$50,000) in 2x11 and 22.5 ($900,000/$40,000) in 2x12. It appears that the small business has a cash deficiency in 2x12, which implies a possible liquidity problem.

You should compute and examine *cash adequacy ratios* as a reflection of the available funds to meet expenses and obligations. Cash flow from operations are the "cash earnings" of the business. Net income backed up by cash is important, since it represents a liquid source of funds. Cash can be used to meet debt payments, buy fixed assets, and other necessary items. The higher the ratio of cash flow from operations to net income, the better.

Cash flow from operations equals:

Net income

Add: Noncash expenses (e.g., depreciation)

Cash flow from operations

Cash reinvestment into the business is a positive sign because it indicates future growth. The *cash reinvestment ratio* equals cash used divided by cash obtained. Cash used equals increases in plant and equipment plus increase in net working capital. (Working capital equals current assets less current liabilities.) Cash obtained equals income after tax plus depreciation.

Cash adequacy may also be looked at in terms of cash flow generated from operations less cash payments required to pay debt principal and capital expenditures.

The *cash-flow-to-total-debt* ratio indicates your ability to pay debts; if you are unable to meet your obligations, you may go out of business! The *ratio of cash plus marketable securities to current assets* (assets having a life of one year or less) indicates the percentage of your current assets that are supported by cash and near-cash assets. These are the most liquid assets of the business and are readily available to pay your bills.

The ratio of cash plus marketable securities to current liabilities (debt due within one year) indicates the immediate amount of cash available to satisfy short-term debt. The more your current debt is covered with cash and near-cash assets, the better your ability to meet supplier and creditor claims.

The ratio of cash plus marketable securities plus receivables divided by the year's cash expenses reveals how many times your immediate liquid resources are sufficient to meet cash expenses. For example, a ratio of five means that you have $5 in liquid assets to cover each dollar in cash expenses. A higher ratio indicates greater protection in paying expenses.

The cash flow to capital expenditures ratio equals cash flow from operations divided by expenditures for plant and equipment. This ratio indicates your ability to maintain plant and equipment from cash earnings rather than from borrowing. You are better off obtaining funds internally from the business because there are no financing costs associated with it.

The cash flow adequacy ratio equals:

$$\frac{\text{Five-year sum of cash flow from operations}}{\text{Five-year sum of capital expenditures and inventory additions}}$$

The purpose of the cash flow adequacy ratio is to determine the degree to which a small business has generated sufficient cash flow from operations to cover capital expenditures and investment in inventories. To remove cyclical and other erratic influences, a five-year total is used in the computation. A ratio of one indicates you have covered your needs based on attained levels of growth without having to resort to external financing. If the ratio drops below one, internally generated cash from operations may be inadequate to maintain current operating growth levels. The ratio also reflects the impact of inflation on fund requirements.

In evaluating cash, you should also note whether a portion is unavailable for use, or "restricted." For example, a compensating balance does not represent "free" cash. For example, a compensating balance does not represent "free" cash. Free cash is money available for use. As previously mentioned, a compensating balance is a deposit a bank can use to offset an unpaid loan.

Cash held as a time deposit or in a temporary escrow account also is not available funds. An escrow account contains money you temporarily deposit with a neutral third party in accordance with a contractual agreement; you have no control over the escrow money until the terms of the contract have been fulfilled. When you sell store furniture and equipment, for example, the buyer might insist that you put escrow money on deposit for three months to reimburse the buyer for any defects requiring repairs to the furniture and equipment.

The ratio of cash plus cash equivalents to working capital looks at cash plus marketable securities having a maturity of three months or less relative to working capital. (The definition of cash equivalents used in this ratio is that defined by the Financial Accounting Standards Board in order to prepare the Statement of Cash Flows- see Key 11.) A high ratio indicates better liquidity, and offers protection to short-term creditors in meeting debt that is coming due in the near future.

Too much cash-- A troubling omen

Big cash stakes generally are a sign that a company is healthy. Big cash stakes can be a troubling omen, too. When big cash balances persist for several quarters, it can be a sign that financial managers don't see growth opportunities. That's not the hallmark of a healthy economy. The key question now: When and how will companies spend the extra money? Broadly speaking, companies can do the following with their cash:

1. Keep it in the bank
2. Pay down debt
3. Buy back own shares
4. Invest in short-term securities
5. Invest in new projects

6. Buy a competitor
7. Pay cash dividends

MODULE 3

Cash Budgeting and Optimal Cash Balances

8 Cash Flow Cycles

A small business dealing in inventory pays cash to buy or produce products and sells the products to receive cash; a service business pays money for employee services and receives money from the clients who receive such services. The cash flow cycle for either is diagrammed below:

Figure 1: The Cash Flow Cycle

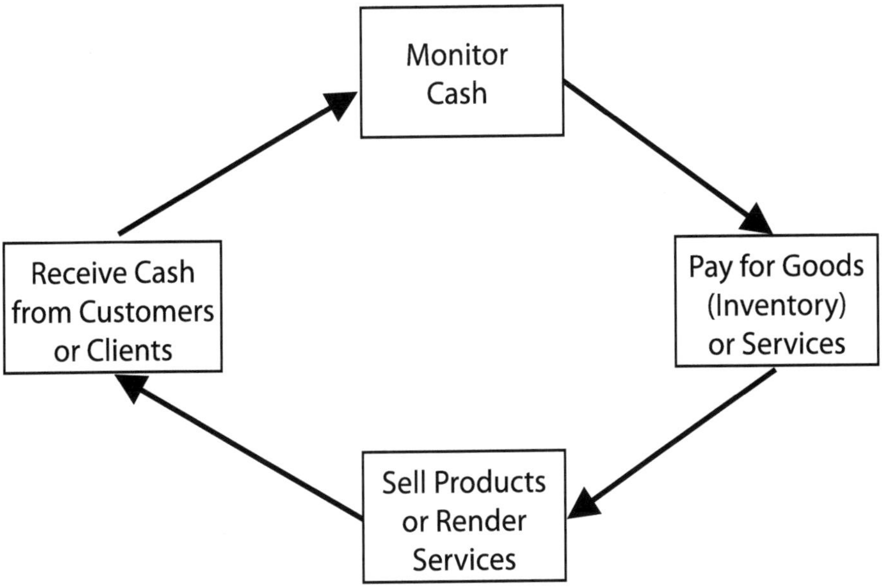

The cash flow cycle differs among small businesses and industries. The cash flow cycle for an appliance store, for example, is different from that of a stationery store.

As previously mentioned, cash inflows include cash sales, collections from customers on account, sale of assets, interest revenue, and rental revenue. Cash outflows include merchandise or material purchases, payroll, fringe benefits, rent, utilities, insurance, taxes, purchase of assets (e.g., store furnishings), and payments to subcontractors.

If collections are not received on time from customers, you may be unable to make payments to suppliers and for operating expenses.

A small business typically pays cash before it receives cash. It makes payments to vendors, employees, the landlord, utilities, etc., before cash is received from customers or clients as payment for merchandise or services. There is usually not a perfect timing of cash receipts and cash payments. This gap in cash may be serviced from an existing cash balance and/or borrowing from a financing institution.

There is less need for a cash balance when cash receipts coincide with the timing of cash payments. An example is when cash collections from customers are received at the end of the month and cash payments to suppliers are also made at the end of the month. Another example is when cash is received from a tenant at the beginning of the month and cash is also paid on loans at the beginning of the month.

You should bill customers and pay your bills on a regular cycle throughout the month. Matching cash inflows and cash outflows:

- Reduces the need for short-term bank loans to bridge the gap between paying money before receiving it.
- Avoids sudden cash surges or shortages.

The cash flow cycle depends on many factors, including vendor credit policy, customer credit terms, the time it takes to receive merchandise from suppliers, how long goods are stored, the payment period, amount of dollar purchases and sales, amount of operating expenses and when they are due, and production period (in the case of a manufacturer). In problem times, cash savings may be achieved by cutting your salary. The lost wages plus a bonus may be recouped when things get better.

9 Determining the Right Cash Balance to Hold

The goal of cash management is to have sufficient cash balances for transactions while avoiding excessive balances. An adequate cash balance is required to carry out the routine transactions of your business and to satisfy unexpected cash demands; if there is significant business activity or volatility in cash flow, you will need a greater cash balance. Excess cash may be used to invest in marketable securities, buy productive assets (such as computers or machinery and equipment), or reduce debt.

The amount of the cash balance held depends upon:

- The *state of the economy*. If economic uncertainty exists, the conservative strategy is to retain higher cash balances.
- *Rate of return that can be earned from marketable securities*. If you can earn a higher rate of return on short-term investments, you should invest cash in them.
- *Uncertainty associated with cash flows*. If you have a high degree of uncertainty in cash inflow, higher cash balances should be held.
- *Length of the planning period*. A short-term period is easier to plan for than a long-term period and allows you to hold less cash balances.
- *How long funds are needed*. If you need funds only for a few days, less cash may be retained.
- *Whether the bank requires time deposits to obtain banking services and lower bank charges*. However, closely monitor bank balances to make sure you are not depositing excessive funds at the bank without receiving an adequate return on your money.

- *Ability to borrow on short notice.* If you are unable to borrow quickly, you will need a higher cash balance as a reserve.
- *Likelihood of sudden, unexpected developments such as fires and lawsuits.* You may have to retain cash balances for an emergency.

If there is an inadequate cash balance, you face the following adverse effects:

- The negative impact on your credit rating of not paying a creditor on time.
- The possibility of losing a cash discount and incurring late fees.
- The inability to make a bargain purchase because of lack of funds.
- The payment of brokerage and administrative fees when marketable securities are sold or a bank line of credit is used to obtain funds.
- The possibility of having to borrow at high interest rates.
- The need to sell assets to derive cash, such as selling accounts receivable to a third party.

Cash inflows can sometimes be matched against cash outflows to reduce the need for a cash reserve; however, a slight timing difference between cash receipts and cash payments may place a drain on liquid resources.

When interest rates are high, you lose a lot of money by not having cash to invest for a return. For example, if the interest rate is 12 percent, $50,000 in cash that is not invested results in lost income per day of $17 ($50,000 x 12% x 1/360).

Overdraft protection allows you to write checks in excess of the actual amount in your checking account. The bank automatically lends you the money to cover the deficit. The advantages of overdraft protection are that you can reduce your cash balance and still avoid having checks "bounce."

A new business has a greater chance of experiencing a cash shortage than an established one. If your business is growing rapidly, you may have cash shortages due to high payments for inventory, fixed assets, and salaries. Your growth will probably be supported with borrowed money.

In a recession, you may be vulnerable to cash flow hardships. Declining sales coupled with increasing costs can eat into profits and cash flows even while it is difficult to borrow and renew loans. If you can borrow, it will be at higher interest rates. Your bills may pile up without your having enough money to pay them.

Time value of money

There is a time value to money. Since today's dollars are worth more than future dollars, try to retain dollars as long as possible. The faster you receive cash, the better, because you can invest the money for a return.

The value of a cash receipt or cash payment depends on the date of the transaction; \$10,000 received today has a greater value than \$10,000 received six months from now.

In making your financial decisions, such as determining annual loan payments or investments accumulation, you may need to use future value and present value tables. You may want to know how much you have to invest each year to have a desired balance to buy store equipment. What is the interest rate you are being charged on a loan? How many years will it be before you can expand to another store? What is the growth rate of the business? Is it worth introducing a new product or service? These are just a few of the many practical applications that the tables offer.

The future (compound) value of money is important to consider in making investment decisions. You can solve for different unknowns, such as accumulated amount, annual amount, interest rate, and number of periods. Here are some guidelines for using future value tables.

- A future value table can be used to determine the future (later) amount of cash paid or received.
- The "Future Value of \$1" table is used if you have unequal cash flows each period or a lump-sum cash flow. (Table 1 in the Appendix)
- The "Future Value of Annuity of \$1" table is used if the cash flows each period are equal and occur at the end of the period. (Table 2 in the Appendix)

Present (discount) value of money is also considered in making decisions.

Different unknowns may be solved for, such as present value amount, annual payment, interest rate, and number of periods. Guidelines for using the tables follow:

- A Present Value table is used if you want to determine the *current* amount of receiving or paying future cash flows.
- The "Present Value of \$1" table is used if you have unequal cash flows each period or a lump-sum cash flow. (Table 3 in the Appendix)
- The "Present Value of Annuity of \$1" table is used if the cash flows are equal each period and paid/received at the end of each period. (Table 4 in the Appendix)

Note: Many financial calculators and spreadsheet packages such as *Excel* allow for the easy application of discounting and compounding cash flow.

As an example, let's say that you expect to receive the following mixed stream of cash inflows over the next three years for a new product.

YEAR	CASH INFLOW
1	$10,000
2	20,000
3	5,000

You earn a minimum of six percent on your money. What is the present value of cash inflows you will receive from this product? You would use the "Present Value of $1" table to figure this out because the cash inflows each year are different.

The present value of this series of mixed streams of cash inflows is as follows:

YEAR	CASH INFLOW	X	PRESENT VALUE FACTOR	=	PRESENT VALUE
1	$10,000	X	0.943	=	$ 9,430
2	20,000	X	0.890	=	17,800
3	5,000	X	0.840	=	4,200
					$31,430

10 Accounting for and Reporting of Cash

Don't mix your personal cash with the cash of your small business; always maintain separate bank accounts for personal and business purposes.

Accounting for cash

Many business transactions involve the receipt and payment of cash. Cash transactions are recorded after proper documentation in either the *cash receipts journal* or the *cash disbursements* (payments) *journal*. If you receive cash, it is recorded in the cash receipts journal; if you pay cash, it is recorded in the cash disbursements journal. Maintaining up-to-date accounting records aids in establishing internal control over cash and provides account figures for financial statement preparation and tax returns.

Documentation of cash transactions includes paid invoices, cancelled checks, sales invoices, cash register tapes, and deposit slips. Documentation should be kept in a safe location and properly filed in case you need to retrieve it.

The cash receipts journal contains a list, updated daily, of cash received, along with an explanation of its source. The cash account is increased and the source of the cash receipt noted (e.g., cash sale, payment from customers, interest income, and dividend income). The small business owner must trace the cash receipts recorded on the books to the deposits recorded on the bank statement to assure they are in agreement. A short illustrative cash receipts journal follows:

Cash Receipts Journal

		CASH	ACCOUNTS RECEIVABLE	SALES	OTHER
Date	Payor	Debit	Credit	Credit	Credit

If your business has over-the-counter cash receipts, occasional errors may occur in making change. Such cash shortages or overages are revealed when the cash count at the end of the day does not agree with the cash register tape.

The cash disbursements journal also contains a list of each day's payments, along with the payee's name and explanation. This listing complements the entries made in your checkbook. Each payment requires a decrease in the cash account. Cash payments may be made for expenditures such as cash purchases of merchandise, payments to suppliers on account, operating expenses, and purchase of assets (e.g., business car). The cash disbursements journal lists the name of the payee, explanation of payment, and check number. An illustrative cash disbursements journal follows:

Cash disbursements journal

			CASH	ACCOUNTS PAYABLE	OTHER
Date	Check Number	Payee	Credit	Debit	Debit

You should pay bills by check in order to have appropriate records; if you pay by cash, make sure you obtain a receipt. The explanation of cash payment should be noted in your records. If the Internal Revenue Service audits you, its agents will want to see both a receipt and a reference in your diary or other suitable place.

After cash transactions are recorded in the cash receipts journal and cash disbursements journal, the cash entries are transferred to the cash account in the *general ledger* so you may obtain your cash balance at any time. This ledger is a separate book containing all of the accounts of the business. You should check the balance at the end of each month to see if you have adequate cash to pay bills and make loan payments in the next month. As a rule of thumb, monthly net cash flow should be at least three times the amount of customer balances.

If you feel you have a lot of money to spend, check with the cash account before committing yourself to a major purchase. An illustrative cash account in the ledger appears below.

Cash

DEBIT	CREDIT

The general ledger also contains a "control account" for accounts receivable and accounts payable. These accounts directly affect cash flow.

In addition to the accounts receivable and accounts payable control accounts, there are separate accounts receivable and accounts payable *subsidiary ledgers* to keep track of the balances of each customer and supplier. The total balance of all customers in the subsidiary accounts receivable ledger should *equal* the accounts receivable balance in the control account in the general ledger.

By looking at the subsidiary accounts receivable ledger, you can see how much each customer owes you and how long the balance has been due. The *accounts receivable subsidiary ledger* includes the customer name, account number, date and terms of purchase, amount of sale, amounts collected, and open balance. At the end of the month, statements are sent to customers showing the balances due. In the *accounts payable subsidiary ledger*, there is a list of amounts you owe suppliers and for how long these amounts have been owing.

Petty cash

In addition to expenditures made through the cash disbursements journal, which are in the form of checks issued to pay vendors and to cover operating expenses, you may have many expenditures of a nominal amount (for items such as postage, supplies, and taxi fare) for which it is impractical to issue checks.

The petty cash fund is established for a fixed amount that is periodically reimbursed by a single check to cover the amounts expended. In establishing and maintaining the petty cash fund, you should follow these procedures:

1. Estimate the total of the small amounts most likely to be paid during a one-month period.
2. Draw and cash a check for the estimated monthly amount, and put the money in the petty cash fund.
3. When money is paid from the petty cash fund, have the recipient prepare and sign a voucher. An explanation should be given for the disbursement. The signed voucher serves as a receipt and provides documentation of the transaction.
4. As a payment is made, enter the voucher in the petty cash record and place it with the balance of money in the petty cash box.
5. At the end of the month, issue and cash a check to replenish the petty cash fund to its original amount.

An illustrative petty cash voucher follows:

Petty Cash Voucher

Number:	Date:
Received by:	Amount:
Explanation:	

The petty cash record takes the following form:

Petty Cash Record

Date	Explanation	Voucher Number	Receipts	Taxi fare	Supplies	Postage

Payroll

One of the largest cash payments a company will make is for employee salaries, which are recorded in the payroll records. The *payroll* information includes employee name and number, social security number, address, telephone number, hourly rate, hours worked, gross salary, tax withheld, other deductions (insurance, pension), and net pay. The payroll record not only supports the cash disbursement for wages, but is required in preparing the payroll tax returns for federal and local taxing agencies. In addition, tax documents (e.g., W-2s) must be mailed to employees at the end of the year for filing with their tax returns.

Reporting cash

Cash includes demand deposits and savings deposits in a bank as well as items the bank will accept for immediate deposit (for example, paper money, coins, checks, money orders). Items *not* considered to be cash are postdated checks, IOUs, postage stamps, and notes receivable. The total of "cash on hand" and "cash on deposit" in the bank is shown in the balance sheet as one figure. Cash is the most liquid of *current assets* (assets having a life of one year or less) and is listed first. As mentioned earlier, *restricted* cash in a bank account (for example, cash held as a compensating balance as collateral for a loan) is not considered a current asset.

11 Statement of Cash Flows

Current profitability is only one important factor in success. Also essential is cash flow. In fact, a profitable business, for example, a business with significant credit sales but with a very long collection period, may have a cash crisis. The business reports a profit but does not have the cash from those sales.

It is important to know your cash flow to adequately plan. Should you cut back on cash payments? Where are you spending your money? What products are cash drains or cash surpluses? Is there enough money to pay bills and buy needed equipment? Are you liquid?

A Statement of Cash Flows is useful because it provides valuable information that is unavailable in the balance sheet and income statement. The statement presents the sources and uses of cash and is a basis for cash flow analysis.

The *Statement of Cash Flows* classifies cash receipts and cash payments from (1) operating, (2) investing, and (3) financing activities. Let's look at each of these major sections:

1. *Operating activities* relates to the manufacturing and selling of goods or the rendering of services. Cash inflows that come from operating activities include (1) cash sales or collections on receivables, and (2) cash receipts from interest income and dividend income. Cash outflows include cash paid for (1) merchandise, and (2) for operating expenses.
2. *Investing activities* relate to the purchase and sale of fixed assets (such as equipment and machinery) and the purchase of stocks and bonds of other businesses. Cash inflows comprise (1) amounts received from selling fixed assets, and (2) receipts from sales of stocks and bonds of other companies. Cash outflows include (1) payments to buy fixed assets, and (2) disbursements to buy stocks and bonds of other companies.

3. *Financing activities* relate to borrowing and repayment thereof and to issuing stock and reacquiring previously issued shares. Cash inflows comprise (1) funds obtained from loans, and (2) funds received from the sale of stock. Cash outflows include (1) paying off debt, and (2) repurchase of stock.

Analysis of cash flows

Cash flow analysis is a valuable tool. The cash flow statement provides information about the way your business generates and uses cash. An analysis of the statement is helpful in appraising past performances, showing why cash flow increased or decreased, as well as looking at future direction, forecasting liquidity trends, and evaluating your ability to pay debt at maturity.

An analysis of the operating section determines the adequacy of cash flow generated from your sales to meet operating expenses. Are you obtaining positive future net cash flows from your daily activities?

In looking at the investing section, an increase in fixed assets indicates expansion and future growth. A contraction in business arising from the sale of fixed assets without adequate replacement is a negative sign.

An evaluation of the financing section reveals your business's ability to obtain financing as well as its ability to pay debt when it is due. The type of financing used affects risks and the cost of obtaining funds.

Let's consider Mr. Jones, who owns a small business that sells appliances. An analysis of the business reveals that profitability and cash flow have improved. This indicates good earnings performance as well as the fact that earnings are backed up by cash. The decrease in accounts receivable may reveal better collection efforts. The increase in accounts payable is a sign that suppliers have confidence in the business and are willing to give interest free financing. The acquisition of land, a building, and furnishings point to a growing business undertaking capital expansion. The long-term loan indicates that part of the financing of assets is through debt. Overall, there was an increase in cash of $22,000 along with a net income of $61,000. This is a favorable sign considering the significant capital expenditures made. The Statement of Cash Flows for his business follows:

CASH FLOW FROM OPERATING ACTIVITIES		
Net Income		$61,000
Add (deduct) items not affecting cash:		
Depreciation expense	$7,000	
Decrease in accounts receivable	5,000	
Increase in prepaid insurance and rent	(2,000)	
Increase in accounts payable	4,000	14,000
Net cash flow from operating activities		75,000
CASH FLOWS FROM INVESTING ACTIVITIES		
Purchase of land	$ (35,000)	
Purchase of store building	(30,000)	
Purchase of store furnishings	(18,000)	(83,000)
CASH FLOWS FROM FINANCING ACTIVITIES		
Long-term loans	30,000	30,000
Net increase in cash		$22,000

The statement of cash flows versus the income statement

The Statement of Cash Flows is different from the income statement. The Statement of Cash Flows presents the cash receipts and cash payments of the business by source. It reveals where cash is coming from and where it is going. The statement emphasizes *cash flows*: its bottom line is the cash balance at the end of the period.

The income statement looks not at cash flows but at the *profitability* of the business. It reveals net income-revenue less expenses. Revenue, which is income earned from operations and may or may not involve cash receipts, is earned from sales of merchandise and the rendering of services. A credit sale is recorded as revenue, although it does not involve receiving money; expenses which are incurred to obtain revenue and may or may not involve cash payment, may result from either conducting operations (e.g., operating expenses) or financing the business (e.g., interest expense). Bills received for accrued expenses during the year (e.g., utilities) reduce profit but do not involve cash payment until such time when these bills are actually paid. For example, a telephone bill covering the month of December 2x11 is an expense for the year 2x11. This expense reduces net income. However, the bill may not be paid until January 2x12.

12 Preparing the Cash Budget

The *cash budget* presents the amount and timing of the expected cash inflow and outflow for a designated time period. It is a tool for cash planning and control and should be detailed so that you know how much is needed to run your business. If you can reliably estimate cash flows, you may retain cash balances near a target level with fewer transactions.

The cash budget should be prepared for the shortest time period for which reliable financial information can be obtained. In the case of many small businesses, this may be one week; however, predicting major cash receipts and cash payments for a specific day is also possible.

The cash budget helps management keep cash balances in a reasonable relationship to needs. It aids in avoiding having unnecessary idle cash as well as averting possible cash shortages. If there is idle cash, you may invest the excess funds in short-term securities such as U.S. Treasury bills and commercial paper to earn a return; if the budget reveals a cash shortage, you can borrow money, cut expenditures, or sell assets. The cash budget ensures that you will have sufficient cash funds available to your business at all times.

The cash budget also allows you to review future cash receipts and cash payments to uncover possible *patterns of cash flows*. In this way, you can study your collection and disbursement efforts to ascertain if you are maximizing your net cash flows. In addition, the cash budget reveals when and how much to borrow and when you will be able to pay the money back. For example, if your cash budget indicates that a significant cash outlay will be needed to buy assets (e.g., store equipment), you may have to borrow money and determine a debt repayment schedule. In order to obtain a line of credit, lenders typically require you to submit the cash budget, along with your financial statements.

The cash budget typically consists of four major sections:

1. The *receipts* section, which is the beginning cash balance, cash collections from customers, and other receipts.

2. The *disbursements* section, which comprises all cash payments that are planned during the budget period.
3. The *cash surplus or deficit* section, which shows the difference between the cash receipts section and the cash disbursements section.
4. The *financing* section, which provides a detailed account of the borrowings and repayments expected during the budgeting period. If additional financing is needed, the cash budget projections allow sufficient lead time for the necessary arrangements to be made.

Cash budgets are often prepared monthly, but there are no strict rules for determining the length of the budget period. As a general rule, it should be long enough to show the effect of your policies in running the small business, yet short enough so that estimates can be made with reasonable accuracy. The following table shows the major components of a cash budget.

Major Cash Flow Components of a Cash Budget

CASH INFLOWS		CASH OUTFLOWS	
Operating:		Operating:	
	Cash sales		Payroll
	Collections		Inventory purchases
			Insurance
			Payments to suppliers
Nonoperating:		Nonoperating:	
	Royalties		Capital expenditures
	Rents		Interest
	Investment income		Loan repayments
	Sale of marketable securities		Tax payments
	Loan proceeds		Purchase of marketable securities

The basis for estimating cash receipts is *sales*, whether from cash sales or collections from customer balances. An incorrect sales estimate will result in erroneous cash estimates. The sales predictions also influence the projected cash outlays for manufacturing costs, since production is tied to sales. The projection of operating expenses may be tied to the suppliers' payment terms.

The following table presents a cash budget for the Johnson Ski Shop. For illustrative purposes, we make the following assumptions:

- The store desires to maintain a $5,000 minimum cash balance at the end of each month.
- The borrowing agreement entered into with the bank calls for borrowing and repayment thereof in multiples of $500.

Johnson Ski Shop
Cash Budget
January through March, 2x11

	JANUARY	FEBRUARY	MARCH
Cash balance, beginning	$10,000	$ 9,401	$ 5,461
Add: Receipts:			
Collections from customers	54,300	57,120	66,080
Total cash available (a)	64,300	66,521	71,541
Less: Disbursements:			
Merchandise	4,549	4,560	4,860
Wages	19,750	18,000	22,250
Supplies	10,650	9,950	11,650
Miscellaneous	15,950	12,750	14,750
Equipment purchase	-	24,300	-
Income tax	4,000	----	---
Total disbursements	54,899	69,560	53,510
Cash balances desired	5,000	5,000	5,000
Total cash required (b)	59,899	74,560	58,510
Cash surplus (deficit) (c) = (a) – (b)	4,401	8,039	13,031
Financing:			
Borrowing	-	8,500	-
Repayment	---	--	(8,500)
Cash Balance, ending	9,401*	5,461**	9,531 ***

* $9,401 = $4,401 (cash surplus) + $5,000 (cash balance desired)

** $5,461 = $8,500 (borrowing) -$8,039 (cash deficit) + $5,000 (cash balance desired)

*** $9,531 = $13,031 (cash surplus) - $8,500 (repayment) + $5,000 (cash balance desired).

Variance analysis

Comparing estimated and actual cash figures allows you to investigate the reasons for any significant discrepancies and to take any needed corrective action. *Variance analysis* allows you to get a better picture of your cash position and provides insight in improving cash estimates in the next budgeting period. It also aids in the periodic revision of projections. This updating typically occurs at the beginning of each budget segment (e.g., the first day of a quarter, assuming you prepare a quarterly budgeting period, or the first day of a month, assuming a monthly budgeting period). Budgets should be adjusted immediately for significant changes. The following table shows an illustrative variance analysis report.

Variance Analysis Report for Cash Budgeting

	BUDGET	ACTUAL	PERCENTAGE CHANGE	EXPLANATION
Cash balance, beginning				
Add: Receipts:				
Collection from customers				
Total cash available				
Less: Disbursements:				
Merchandise				
Wages				
Supplies				
Miscellaneous				
Equipment purchase				
Income tax				
Total Disbursements				
Cash balance, ending				

Variance analysis is crucial for a small business whether it be a retailer, wholesaler, manufacturer, or service concern. Evaluation of cash variances may be done yearly, quarterly, monthly, or daily. If cash theft is suspected, variance analysis would of course be done more frequently. Cash is the easiest asset to steal.

13 Revenues and Expenses

The income statement reports the profitability of a business over a specified *time period*. Therefore, it is necessary to reflect revenue and expense items applicable to that period.

Under *accrual* accounting, revenue is recognized when *earned* at the time of sale or rendering of services. Expenses are recognized when incurred and are matched against the revenue to which they are directly related; however, accrual accounting for revenue and expense does not necessarily affect cash flow.

When looking at cash flow you must consider only revenue that involves cash receipts and expenses that involve cash payments.

In other words, consider revenue and expenses when they are received or disbursed, rather than when they are earned or incurred. Examples of cash revenue are cash sales, cash received from customers at the time professional services are performed, and cash received for interest income. Examples of cash expenses are salaries paid, rent paid, and postage paid.

A company may show a net income but have a cash crisis if that net income is not supported by cash earnings (cash flow from operations). Hence, consideration should be given only to revenue sources and expense incurrences directly affecting cash flow.

Cash flow from operations may be computed either by subtracting cash expenses from cash revenue or by adjusting net income for noncash items, as follows:

Accrual-based net income

Add: Noncash expenses (e.g., depreciation)

Less: Noncash revenue (e.g., amortization of deferred revenue)

Cash flow from operations

Suppose, for example, that the net income from your business was $150,000 for the year. All of your expenses were paid with cash except for depreciation of $10,000. The only noncash source of income was $2,000. The cash flow from operations equals:

Net Income	$150,000
Add: Depreciation	10,000
Less: Noncash revenue	(2,000)
Cash flow from operations	$158,000

Reducing expenses to save cash

The proper management of expenses may reduce your cash outlays by cutting costs. You should determine which expenses are fixed (inflexible) and which are variable (flexible). Fixed expenses are the same each month (e.g., insurance, rent) and are typically provided by a written agreement. Since fixed expenses are inflexible, you have very little control over them in the short run. Variable expenses may fluctuate each month (e.g., direct materials, direct labor, supplies). Because variable expenses are flexible, you have some control over them in the short-term.

You may want to ask the following questions:

- What amount of each expense is discretionary (e.g., can be changed at will, such as promotion and entertainment)?
- What expenses are excessive (e.g., lavish office furnishings, Mercedes-Benz company car)?
- What expenses can be eliminated (e.g., charitable contributions)?

Recurring expenses (e.g., salaries, rent) may not be easily reduced, whereas nonrecurring expenses (e.g., office parties, entertainment, out-of-town travel) may be easily reduced.

It may be advisable to use an *Expense Book* to record and control business expenses. Recording such costs in one place may make it easier for you to examine them closely for areas where reductions are possible.

MODULE 4

Internal Control

14 Internal Control over Cash

Cash receipts originate from many sources, for example, from customers on account, from cash sales for merchandise or services, and from miscellaneous sources, such as interest on bank accounts and dividends on investments. In some small businesses, cash receipts are in the form of checks received by mail. As mentioned earlier in Key 10, all cash receipts should be recorded and deposited daily. The risk of losing checks or cash increases with the amount of time they remain on your premises. Checks to be deposited should be endorsed "For Deposit Only."

Cash receipt documents should be prenumbered. Duties should be segregated between the employee who physically handles the money and the employee who keeps the records. This segregation not only allows one employee to check another employee's work, but also guards against theft. Because checks received payable to the company may be stolen by an employee and because the misappropriation is more likely before the checks are recorded than after, concealment is easier. A wise internal control procedure is to have one employee who is independent of the processor of cash prepare a list of cash receipts before they are processed. Subsequently, you can compare this list to the cash receipts recorded in the records and deposited. In any event, employees having custody of cash should be bonded.

Persons handling cash receipts should not have access to, or authority over, customer records, nor should they be allowed to prepare bank reconciliations or post transactions from the journal ledger.

In the case of cash sales, the sale should be entered in the cash register, and there should exist separate documentation (e.g., restaurant check). A modern cash register should be used, and it should display the amount of the cash transaction. The customer should also be encouraged to obtain a cash register receipt. In fact, some businesses promise the customer the merchandise or services free if he or she does not receive a receipt. The cash register should provide locked-in totals that you can compare with the related bank deposit.

You have to be on guard against possible *embezzlement*, which occurs when an employee pockets money without recording the sale. Embezzlement may be indicated by the following:

- Unexplained shortages in merchandise.
- Delays in depositing money at the bank.
- Collection delays.

Talk to employees about their personal financial problems to see if you can help them. In this way, you may reduce the temptation to steal money. As a precautionary measure, modify or rotate their job assignments relating to handling money.

You should make all disbursements by check and only for goods and services that are known to have been received and for other authorized purposes. Payments should be made only *after* proper documentation and approval are obtained.

The primary document supporting a disbursement is the vendor's invoice. Before the invoice is paid, it should be checked for mathematical accuracy. The invoice should also be compared to the purchase order and receiving report. Employees checking the invoice for correctness should sign or initial the document after they are satisfied with it. Investigate differences.

In the case of operating expenses, a memorandum of approval or a check request should be issued before payment.

Internal control over cash disbursements requires that the disbursing function be subdivided between preparing, signing, and distributing each check. Checks should be prepared *after* the related documentation has been properly approved. The name of the payee should be indicated on the check. A check payable to cash or bearer should not be issued since it may be cashed by anyone. Consecutively number checks. The use of a check protector (a device that imprints the dollar amount on the check face mechanically) helps to prevent alteration of the amount on the check.

Checks should only be signed by you. Never sign a blank check; a dishonest bookkeeper can fill in a fraudulent payee and amount. After the check is signed, the invoice, or supporting documentation, should be stamped "paid" or otherwise cancelled to prevent its reuse. One of the authors, who is a certified public accountant, knows of cases in which bookkeepers embezzled money by improperly making out and signing checks. In one case, the owner signed blank checks that were later improperly filled out by the bookkeeper; in another case, the client signed checks without first carefully reviewing them.

Checks written in excess of a specified dollar amount may require two signatures. While smaller checks may be signed mechanically, larger checks should be manually signed.

After a check has been signed, it should be mailed or given directly to the payee by the signer. The check should not be returned to an employee who has participated in the check-processing function in order to prevent the employee from retrieving a check representing an improper disbursement.

There should be a separation of duties in payroll between people who prepare the payroll and physically issue checks.

Finally, the bookkeeper should take a vacation at least once a year so another employee who fills in during that time can note any suspicious activities.

15 Audit of the Cash Account and Payment System

Cash can easily be stolen. Make sure cash balances reflect all cash and cash items on hand, in transit, or on deposit with banks. Also, make sure that cash balances are properly classified in the balance sheet and that any restrictions on the availability of cash are properly disclosed. A lender may sue you for misstating cash on a loan application.

The following audit procedures may be employed by you and/or a responsible party to ensure the accuracy of the cash account:

- Conduct surprise counts of petty cash and cash receipts. Also, investigate whether petty cash has been stolen through the issuance of false vouchers. Prenumber petty cash vouchers.
- Estimate the amount of cash that should have been recorded; compare it to cash receipts.
- Note delays in depositing cash.
- Identify cashiers who omit items or undercharge when ringing up sales, since they may be giving merchandise away free or at reduced cost to friends or be receiving a kickback.
- Watch out for cashiers who repeatedly have a cash shortage.
- Determine if popular waiters or waitresses are requested because they are giving food away in order to receive better tips.
- Hire "shopper detectives" who pretend to be customers to see if employees are stealing money or are undercharging customers.

- Determine if salespeople are charging customers too little in return for favors.
- Note unusual activity in an inactive account, since it may indicate cash is being stolen.
- Confirm that proper insurance protection (employee bonding) exists for those who handle cash so that you will be reimbursed in the event of loss.
- Immediately look into customer complaints involving an order not received even though payment was made.
- Investigate an unusual decrease in sales, which may signal that sales are not being recorded and money is being pocketed by employees.
- Investigate an increase in sales returns, because it may indicate receipts are being concealed.
- Be sure that the person handling cash receipts is different from the person recording cash payments.
- Watch for the removal of cash and the substitution of an improper receipt (e.g., merchandise return slip).
- Arrange for bank statements and deposit slips to be returned to an employee other than the one who made the deposit.
- Be alert for cash payments to vendors when no liability exists. This may indicate fraud.
- Match payees to the list of approved vendors and note any discrepancies.
- Investigate whether company checks are being issued to nonexistent vendors for fraudulent bills.
- Review changes in the amounts due to vendors.
- Prepare a monthly bank reconciliation proving that the balance per books equals the balance per bank. (See Key 30.)
- List and investigate (e.g., by reference to supporting detail and proper authorization) all unusual cancelled checks, such as those payable to cash, former employees, and friends. Further, review third-party endorsements.
- Investigate the possibility of employees forging company checks payable to their order and then discarding the checks when they are returned from the bank. Verify all checks for proper signature.
- Investigate the write-off of customers' accounts. Perhaps the money was received by the employee who wrote off the account as uncollectible.

- Bank charge-backs should be received directly from the bank and investigated by a person independent of the one physically handling collections.
- Checks received should be restrictively endorsed for deposit only to the company's bank account.
- If cash registers are used, a copy of the tape should be given to the customer as a receipt.
- Instruct the bank not to cash checks drawn to the order of the company.
- Disbursements other than by petty cash should be made by check.

MODULE 5

Cash Forecasting and "What-if" Analysis

16 Cash Forecasting

Accurate cash forecasting is crucial for the success of small businesses. Cash forecasting is valuable in projecting financial needs, identifying areas of financial strength or deficiency, formulating a realistic timetable to achieve goals, and comparing expectations to actual results. Once you know your expected cash position, you can plan expenditures, such as asset acquisitions, debt repayment, operating expenses, such as advertising, and wage settlements.

In deciding upon the forecasting period to use, consider the nature of your operation. If you have stable sales, a quarterly forecast is suitable. On the other hand, if your sales are unstable, a monthly forecast will help you keep on top of things. The forecasting period also depends on your exposure to economic conditions and the business cycle; for example, if you are subject to three months' seasonality, a quarterly forecasting period is called for.

Your cash forecast should cover both the peak and ebb points of sales for the year. For example, cash forecast for a toy store or gift shop would be misleading if it did not take into account Christmas sales along with projected sales during the slowest part of the year. The seasonality of the business is crucial in making projections.

As a rule of thumb, avoid making large payments (e.g., operating expenses, debt repayment) at the low point in the cash cycle.

There are two types of forecasts-short-term and long-term. A short-term forecast typically covers one year or less, while a long-term forecast covers more than one year. A long-term forecast is simply an extension of a short-term forecast.

A short-term forecast is more detailed and reliable than a long-term forecast because the short time horizon makes projections easier. A short-term forecast tells you whether you can carry on financial and operating activities over the next year and is crucial if you are experiencing cash problems or significant variability in cash. Will you need a short-term loan? When can you repay it? Do you have excess cash to invest? It is crucial for a small business to have a short-term forecast because of the need for tight control over cash.

The steps in constructing a short-term forecast are as follows:

1. Take into account temporary fluctuations in cash flow.
2. Select a representative period to depict cash flows, such as quarterly or monthly.
3. Plan for unusual cash receipts and cash payments.

A new small business should start off with a monthly forecast broken down by weeks because control is essential in the early stages. Once the business matures, a quarterly forecast broken down by months is adequate.

The benefits to short-term forecasting include:

- Providing the basis for the long-term forecast.
- Providing scheduling loan repayments.
- Timing cash flow to take advantage of cash discounts for early payment to suppliers.
- Timing of borrowings so as to lower financing costs.

A long-term cash forecast shows major acquisitions of assets, major disposals of assets, planned debt financing, and the introduction of new products and/or services. It also provides a basis for judging whether there are adequate net cash inflows to support growth.

17 Forecasting Cash Collections

A forecast of cash collections and potential write-offs of customer balances is essential in cash budgeting. The critical step in making such a forecast is estimating the cash collection and bad debt percentages and applying them to sales or accounts receivable balances. An example follows:

Example

The following data are given for Sharpe's Clothing Store:

	SEPTEMBER ACTUAL	OCTOBER ACTUAL	NOVEMBER ACTUAL	DECEMBER ACTUAL
Cash sales	$ 7,000	$ 6,000	$ 8,000	$ 6,000
Credit sales	50,000	48,000	62,000	80,000

Past experience based on the aging of accounts receivable indicates collection normally occurs in the following pattern:

- No collections are made in the month of sale.
- 80% of the sales of any month are collected in the following month.
- 19% of sales are collected in the second following month.
- 1% of sales are uncollectible.

The total cash receipts for November and December are computed as follows:

	NOVEMBER	DECEMBER
Cash receipts		
Cash sales	$ 8,000	$ 6,000
Cash collections		
September sales		
$50,000 x 19%	9,500	
October sales		
$48,000 x 80%	38,400	
$48,000 x 19%		9,120
November sales		
$62,000 x 80%		49,600
Total cash receipts	$55,900	$64,720

18 What-if Analysis

The cash budget would be incomplete if it were based on only one set of estimated cash inflows and outflows. These figures may well be *expected* cash flows or even most likely estimates, but we need to consider the possibility of errors or variability in cash flow estimates. The following table provides a list of the major certain and uncertain cash flows.

Certain and uncertain cash flows

CERTAIN CASH FLOWS	UNCERTAIN CASH FLOWS
Interest receipts	Cash sales
Rents	Collections
Payroll	Payable payments
Tax payments	
Interest payments	
Loan repayments	

The variability in cash flows can be handled through "what-if" analysis or through optimistic/pessimistic forecasts. For example, what if your cash sales were, say, 10% higher or lower than originally expected? "What-if" analysis typically can be done with the aid of a spreadsheet program such as Excel.

We also have to consider "best/worst-case" scenarios for cash flow forecasting. In a worst-case scenario, a forecast is prepared using the most conservative assumption, for example, low or no growth in sales or the highest expected debt rate. The best-case scenario is based on the most aggressive (optimistic) assumptions, for example, the most optimistic sales growth and the lowest interest rates on debt. This kind of forecasting is important because extreme deviations from expectations are the very circumstances for which you should have contingency plans. This is especially true on the pessimistic side. A cash budget prepared with a worst-case scenario can be quite useful if a crunch does occur. It also enables you to plan for difficult times at a time when you are under less pressure and can weigh all your options carefully and thoughtfully.

"What-if" evaluations consider the best and worst possibilities and also aid in cash planning and decision making since many alternatives are considered. The owner needs flexibility to adjust to changing economic and competitive conditions in the marketplace.

19 Cash Flow Software

Computer software makes it easier for you to manage cash on a day-to-day basis, determine cash balances, plan and analyze cash flows, find cash shortages, invest cash surpluses, account for cash transactions, automate accounts receivable and payable, and do banking by phone. Computerization improves availability, accuracy, timeliness, and monitoring of cash information at minimal cost.

Daily cash information aids in planning how to use cash balances and enables the integration of different kinds of related cash information such as collections on customer accounts and cash balances or the effect of cash payments on cash balances.

Spreadsheet program software such as Microsoft's *Excel*, *Lotus 1-2-3*, and *Quattro Pro* can assist you in developing cash budgets and answering a variety of "what-if" questions. For example, you can see the effect on cash flow of different scenarios (e.g., the purchase and sale of different product lines).

1. Quicken (http://quicken.intuit.com/)

This program is a fast, easy to use, inexpensive accounting program that can help a small business manage its cash flow. Bills can be recorded as postdated transactions when they arrive; the program's *Billminder* feature automatically reminds the payer when bills are due, then, checks can be printed for due bills with a few mouse and/or keystrokes. Similarly, he/she can record invoices and track aged receivables. Together, these features help maximize cash on hand.

2. Up Your Cash Flow XT (www.cashplan.com/)

Up Your Cash Flow XT creates financial forecasts for small to mid-size businesses with many features. This program automatically prepares spreadsheets for profit/loss forecasts, cash flow budgets, projected balance sheet, payroll analysis, term loan amortization schedule, sales/cost of sales by product, ratio analysis, and graphs. Accountants and consultants can use this software to provide management advice, secure financing, assist troubled businesses and offer other valuable services. CFOs, controllers and financial managers use Up Your Cash Flow XT to make fast company budgets, manage cash flow and reach desired levels of profitability. Over 30 reports show the impact of Sales, Expenses, Cost of Sales, Financing, Payroll, Inventory and more. You can run "what-if" scenarios to see how changes in business activity affect the bottom line and compare plan to actual data to measure how close you've come to your goals and be able to predict any cash shortfalls before they happen.

3. Cashflow Plan – Cashflow Forecast Software (www.planware.org/cashshareware.htm?)

Cashflow Plan is a range of powerful, easy-to-use software packages for preparing comprehensive monthly cashflow projections for 12 months ahead. You can use it for cashflow planning, budgets, business planning, fund raising etc. for young & established businesses of all sizes and types. It incorporates a roll-forward facility to help you to speedily update the projections every month. More powerful versions also include a tool for consolidating projections. Cashflow Plan will help plan your business's cash requirements, improve control over cash flows and conserve cash resources. It will be especially useful if you need to forecast cash flows in the context of:

- Tight cash/profit margins
- Limited financial resources
- Planning for growth or radical change
- Compiling cash budgets
- Preparing business improvement plans

Cashflow Plan is pre-formatted to handle the very wide range of the variables and functions normally encountered when preparing cashflow and financial projections. Based on your assumptions, it compiles detailed, fully-integrated financial projections for the coming year on a monthly basis, and for the initial three months on a weekly basis. It automatically produces 20+ pro-forma financial and management reports together with numerous graphs for key variables.

MODULE 6

Managing Payables

20 A Well-Managed Accounts Payable System

An *accounts payable system* should be given the same attention that other key systems contributing to a small business's cash-flow base receive. Accounts payable is just as important as bill collection, inventory management, money management, and credit management.

The control of the cash that *leaves* your company is every bit as important as the cash that comes in through sales and collection efforts. To achieve control, accounts payable must be *aggressively managed* in accordance with the owner's financial status and goals. Bill payments must be planned, not simply made. Payables should be viewed as a flexible system that you can manipulate in response to other factors, such as sales decreases or slowdown in collections.

While there is no such thing as a single accounts payable system that will work for every business, there are nine general rules that well-managed systems should adhere to:

1. *Evaluate cash flow.* Every accounts payable strategy should be rooted in your current cash flow realities. To some degree, that's common sense: If it takes 90 days to collect accounts receivable, it's financially self-destructive for you to pay bills within 15 days. How long does it take dollars spent to be replaced? You should *monitor your cash-to-cash cycle*. Your cash-to-cash cycle is the length of time that elapses from your expenditure of dollars on inventory to the receipt of cash from sales. Take, for instance, a retailer who buys a product on January 1 and pays for it on January 30: it takes him or her 60 days from that point to sell that product (which brings us to March 31)

and 45 days after that to collect the cash (May 15). The cash-to-cash cycle adds up to 105 days, which is the length of time the retailer is in the hole after expending the cash.

Anything a small business owner can do to reduce the number of days in the cash cycle will help the cash flow of that business. Some ways to do this include collecting money from customers faster, selling and distributing faster, and increasing the number of days that the owner takes to pay the bills.

2. *Set goals.* Once you've evaluated your cash flow, establish written payment goals so there can be no confusion among your billpayers. Avoid a situation in which your clerks decide which bills are to be paid and when. Usually, suppliers who yell the loudest are paid the fastest, regardless of overall benefit to the business.

   The payment of bills should be timed to coordinate exactly with your formal disbursement goals. This means you should date checks no earlier than the dates upon which payments are due (and suppliers should receive checks no more than a day or two earlier than the due date). At all times, your goal should be to hold cash in interest-bearing accounts until the last possible minute and still maintain good relations with your suppliers.

3. *Establish payment priorities.* You should set up a two-tiered list of payment priorities, which then becomes part of your formal payment strategy. Tier one, the group that should be paid at all costs and at whatever terms have been agreed upon, should include major vendors and service suppliers, bankers, and, most important, state and federal tax authorities. Tier two, which offers more room for short-term maneuvering during cash flow crunches, should include minor suppliers whose goodwill is less vital to the overall well-being of your business. To avoid confusion, inform the bookkeeper in writing of payment priorities, by supplier.

4. *Aggressively negotiate payment.* Granted, there's not much room for negotiation with bankers or tax collectors, but once they're taken care of, everything else on the payables front should be open for discussion. You have leverage to negotiate better-than-usual terms from your major suppliers, especially during recessionary times, when everyone is afraid of losing business. You should figure out your optimal payment terms (using the cash-to-cash or other cash-flow information as a guide). Then, when orders are placed, not when bills become due or overdue, *negotiate* to achieve those terms.

5. *Forecast cash needs.* You should be able to predict exactly how much cash you will need-and when-to fulfill your payables obligations. That forecast

then becomes an important tool in averting cash flow problems. You should be able to tell if funds will be available at the right time from bank accounts or bank credit lines. If funds will not be available, you can take precautionary measures, such as stepping up customer collection efforts.

6. *Keep good payables records.* Payables records include weekly updates about the aging of every outstanding bill; documentation that matches each bill paid with its original sales order, delivery records, and payment invoice; and total cost records, including interest penalties paid on each bill. The last is important because most owners don't realize how much having to pay interest charges to finance late payables adds to their cost of doing business.
7. *Review payables records regularly.* Payables reports are every bit as important as other cash flow documents and need to be evaluated. Generally speaking, you should review payables--aging schedules weekly. Cost records can be evaluated monthly.
8. *Recognize warning signs.* Since cash flow cycles vary even in the best of times, there may be periods when your payables get stretched without any long-term risk; however, it's essential for you to keep an eye out for indications of more serious problems. One approach is to draw up a "payables problems" checklist that breaks down average bill age, promptness of tax payments, any interest charges, and other warning factors you come up with for your business.
9. *Fraud-proof the payables operation.* You should never underestimate the importance of installing safeguards to prevent your bookkeeper or other employees from looting payables. Fraud can be one of the most common problems a growing small business may encounter in its accounts payable operations.

   To minimize the risks, you should formalize payment procedures that include doublechecks at each step of the process. Bills should be paid only when they can be matched against purchase orders and delivery confirmations, and the bookkeeper should write the check but you should sign it. You should keep blank checks under lock and key and track all numbers, including voided checks. If you make payments by wire transfer, establish bank procedures that ensure proper control over such transfers. The best defense of all against fraud-and it's one that an amazing number of small businesses overlook-is to make certain the checkbook balances each month (see Key 30).

21 Managing Payables

Sound management of accounts payable follows these principles:

- *Prioritize*: Financial obligations fall into three categories: bills to be paid as soon as they're due (wages and salaries, bank loans, and taxes); bills to be paid within 15 days (to professional contractors for services already performed); and bills that should if at all possible be paid within 30 days (all others). As your business begins to feel pinched, perhaps because of an economic downturn, you try to stretch that third category out to 45 to 60 days. When you look at your cash flow, accounts payable are something that you have got some control over-and you will negotiate with suppliers if and when you have to.
- *Negotiate*: You might prefer to negotiate longer payment terms in advance, although this process can be time-consuming. You should telephone major vendors to ask when they absolutely have to have their money. This information should then get recorded in each vendor's accounts payable file. It sets the guidelines for payment of all major outstanding obligations. (With smaller suppliers, there may not be much potential payoff from stretching out payments.)
- *Monitor payables closely*: Each week, analyze an accounts payable aging schedule along with other cash flow documents. As a last resort, use your credit line to make payments if you can't bring the money in fast enough from customer collections.
- *Demonstrate good faith*: When your money doesn't come in, you're in a jam. One possible solution: Pay only *absolute essentials* such as salaries, rent, taxes, and loans. These expenditures cannot be delayed. Employees want to get paid, otherwise, they may strike. Your landlord will evict you if you do not pay the rent. If you do not pay taxes to the Internal Revenue Service, it will close your business. Then you can pay whatever cash is left over to

your vendors. Suppliers are more tolerant, understanding, and flexible since they need your business. Try to pay more money to the more demanding vendors and less to those that are more likely to wait; a partial payment will show vendors that you are trying to repay them. Don't just send the money, get on the phone and explain what's happening and why and set up an informal payment schedule on the spot. Let the vendors know when they can expect to receive the remaining balance. A follow-up letter should also be sent to confirm the telephone conversation. In this way, vendors will know you are serious, because you have put it in writing.

- *Protect credit ratings*: If you can borrow money or have sufficient line of credit, try to protect your credit rating by paying lenders. You do not want to damage your credit standing, because if you do you will be unable to get credit in the future to operate your business. You should look elsewhere to cut spending; for example, stop drawing your own salary if you are an owner. If you pay yourself less, your business credit rating will not be affected. During tough times, particularly, it's more important than ever not to spend what you don't have. You are better off being around to enjoy the economic turnaround that will occur sooner or later.

22 Warning Signs of Payables

Is your business heading for accounts payable problems? Here are five typical symptoms.

- *Aged payables:* Chances are that you are heading for trouble when you start paying bills an average of 45 to 60 days late. (The only exception-bills whose issuers have approved late payment terms without interest penalties, at the time of order).
- *Interest penalties:* Cash-savvy small business owners never box themselves into paying interest charges on overdue bills--unless they've already calculated clear financial benefits from using their funds elsewhere. Once you're paying penalties to even one or two vendors on a regular monthly basis, you're in trouble. Instead, you should approach your creditors about a workout plan that will reduce or perhaps eliminate hefty interest charges.
- *Disorganization:* You know you are in trouble when unpaid bills get thrown into someone's desk instead of entered into a record-keeping system that will keep aging bills so that you can track their payment.
- *Overdue taxes:* Overlooking tax payment-even with the best of intentions-is a sure road to disaster. If your payroll, corporate, federal, or state taxes are late, pay them immediately, even if it means keeping vendors waiting. If you dispute your tax bill, pay it anyway and then fight for a refund; that's the only way to eliminate the risk of costly penalties and interest charges. You may also face civil and criminal penalties if you fail to pay taxes by the due date, underreport income, or pad (overstate) expenses.
- *Hassles from creditors:* Make it a habit to communicate informally with your creditors whenever you think a cash flow crunch *might* be developing. Creditors generally understand if you have good intentions and are forthright.

In auditing payables, do the following:

- Pay only for authorized goods that have been received in good condition.
- Assure duplicate payments have not been made.
- Vendors' invoices should be processed by a person independent of the purchasing and receiving functions.
- A paid invoice should be stamped.
- Compare vendors' invoices to receiving reports.

23 Utilizing Vendor Statement Forms

You may be able to save money by getting to know the policies of your vendors and suppliers. Probe them for the best prices and terms available. You should ask them to fill out an information sheet that forces them to write down the terms and conditions of their sales plans. Once they've completed this form, their verbal promises become written promises. Design a personalized form by putting your business name at the top. Then list the information you need. The following is a list of suggested questions:

1. Vendor's name, address, and phone number (Will he/she accept collect calls? Call 800 information 1(800)555-1212 to find out)
2. Sales representative's name and phone number
3. Amount of minimum purchase
4. Quantity discounts? How much?
5. Advertising/promotion allowances
6. Are extended payment terms available?
7. Delivery terms
8. Service availability
9. Policies on returns for defective goods (Who pays the freight?)
10. Credit term (How flexible is it?)
11. Support for grand opening (Will vendor donate prize or any other support?)

12. Vendor's signature, the date, and an agreement to notify you of any changes in prices and terms

This is a starter. You should be able to negotiate more favorable terms with some vendors. Start by asking open-ended questions such as, "What else can you do for me?" and follow up on the response.

Are the vendors reliable and honest? Check with the Better Business Bureau and industry associations.

Ask vendors for references and check with their other customers.

Are the customers satisfied with the quality of merchandise received, delivery schedules, and service provided?

MODULE 7

Collection and Credit Management

24 Cash Acceleration Strategies

The speed of customer remissions may be accelerated by the use of *return envelopes* with bar codes, nine-digit code numbers, or post office box numbers. *Accelerated Reply Mail* (ARM) is the assignment of a unique "truncating" ZIP code to payments, such as lockbox receivables. The coded remittances are removed from the postal system and processed by banks or third parties. Another suggestion is to send customers preaddressed , stamped envelopes.

Cash receipts may be accelerated by sending out bills to customers at the time the order is shipped. The sooner a customer receives the bill, the sooner he or she is likely to pay. Cash receipt is also hastened by sending out individual invoices rather than monthly statements. Invoice errors should be corrected immediately since the customer will not pay a bill until it is correct.

Require deposits on large or custom orders or progress billings as the work progresses. You should have a system to handle seasonal peak loads to avoid invoicing delays.

You may receive cash faster by allowing the use of merchant credit cards (e.g., VISA, MasterCard); however, banks usually assess a 3% charge on each sale paid for with these cards.

To expedite collection, it is advisable to charge interest on accounts receivable that are past due. If the customer has a financial problem, ask for a postdated check so that you can have first claim on his or her funds when they become available.

You may be able to obtain discounts for early payment or cash-on-delivery payment. As an example, a customer buys $3,000 of merchandise on terms of 2/10, net/30. This means that if the customer makes payment within 10 days of purchase, he or she receives a 2% discount; however, if the customer pays after 10 days have elapsed, full payment is due within 30 days. The discount for early payment in this case is $60

(2% x $3,000), and the net amount the small business will receive is $2,940 ($3,000-$60).

Make sure your small business is fully operational and equipped during seasonal surges. For example, many retailers obtain about 25% of their cash inflow during the Christmas and Chanukah season; it's important to avoid losing potential customers because you have run out of stock on a popular item.

You may decide to use a cash vault service if you are handling substantial amounts of money. In such a system, an armored carrier picks up the collection and deposits it directly to a cash vault for credit. These deliveries may be made and accepted by the bank after normal hours.

25 Property, Plant and Equipment

Purchasing fixed assets such as property, plant, and equipment significantly drains a firm's cash flow. Cash is reduced by both the "down payment" and all subsequent installment payments.

Cash flow is impacted by two aspects of fixed assets:

1. Costs related to existing fixed assets
2. Costs related to expected purchases during the budget period

The *cash outflows* associated with these two areas can be further categorized into the following:

1. Costs associated with owned fixed assets
2. Costs associated with leased fixed assets

Costs associated with owned fixed assets

A checklist of costs for each owned asset should be prepared in order to anticipate all outlays. This checklist should include a description of possible expected expenses. Typical examples of these expenses may include:

1. Repairs and maintenance
   a. *Scheduled* or routine maintenance (protective maintenance)
   b. *Unscheduled* repairs of broken or damaged assets
2. Property taxes
   a. Due semiannually
   b. Due annually
3. Insurance
   a. Three-year policy paid in advance
   b. Three-year policy paid annually
   c. One-year policy paid annually, semiannually, quarterly, or monthly

Costs associated with leased fixed assets

The costs related to leased assets are usually the easiest to project since they represent fixed payments on scheduled dates. Prepare a list of all required payments after a review of each lease. A typical list of cash outlays includes:

- Lease payments
- Repairs and maintenance
- Insurance
- Usage charges (e.g., fee per copy charged for use of a copy machine)
- Supplies

Past invoices often supply much of the needed forecast information about these items.

Leasing rather than buying a fixed asset does not tie up a business's cash for a long time period. A small business may even sell property and then lease it back in order to obtain cash.

Costs associated with expected acquisitions of fixed assets

The expected acquisition of fixed assets involves a purchase or lease. The effect of such a decision significantly impacts the cash flow forecast. Possible impacts on the cash forecast include:

- Cash outlay for a down payment
- Debt or lease payments
- Repairs and maintenance expenditures
- Insurance payments
- Property taxes

Keep in mind that depreciation is a noncash expense and, as such, does not affect cash flow (ignoring taxes). If taxes are considered, depreciation results in a cash savings. For example, if depreciation is $10,000 and the tax rate is 40%, the tax savings is $4,000 ($10,000 x .40). In any event, depreciation is an expense that reduces net income.

26 Delaying Cash Payments for Purchases, Expenses and Payroll

Here are some tactics for delaying payments. *Centralize* the payables' operation so that debt is paid at the most profitable time and the amount of disbursement float (see Key 31) in the system may be ascertained. "Centralization"--having only one center responsible for making payments--facilitates control and record keeping.

Consider staggering payments during the month to level out the cash balance. For example, if you pay suppliers on the tenth and make loan payments on the twentieth, schedule salary checks on the thirtieth of the month.

Put bills on a priority list indicating who should get paid first and who should get paid last. Base the issuance of checks on individual circumstances instead of mailing all checks at the same time.

Mail payments late in the day or on Fridays. Mail from post offices with limited service or where mail has to go through numerous handling points. If float is properly utilized (see Key 31), you can maintain higher bank balances than your actual lower checkbook balances. If you write checks averaging $200 per day and it takes three days for them to clear, you will show a checking balance $600 less than the bank's records.

How can you estimate when checks will clear? For example, if you write out a check on July 1, but you expect it to clear on July 8, deposit the funds on July 7. In this way, you have the use of the money for more days of interest. To be on the safe side, deposit funds a few days before the expected time the check will be deposited at the bank (e.g., July 5).

Payment to suppliers

Payments to vendors should be delayed as long as possible, provided there is no associated finance charge or impairment to your credit rating. Suppliers often grant a grace period. Bills should not be paid before their due dates unless a special discount is given. If there is a discount option, pay the last minute before the discount expires.

Instead of making a full payment on an invoice, make partial payments to delay disbursements. Also, delay payment by requesting additional information about an invoice form the vendor before paying it. Another way to delay payment is to postdate the check.

Use credit cards and charge accounts in order to lengthen the time between the acquisition of goods and the date of payment. In selecting a credit card, consider the interest rate charged, annual fees, grace period (how many days you have to pay for the charges before being charged interest), transaction fee and other fees (e.g., late payment charges, charges for exceeding the credit limit).

Inventory delivery schedules should be as late as possible to delay paying suppliers' invoices. Further, be careful not to overstock, since carrying excess inventory ties up money.

Payment for expenses

Avoid prepaying expenses. For example, if you are going to prepay insurance, do it for one year, not three.

Cost reduction programs also save money. In any event, avoid paying for nonessential items.

A barter arrangement may help to avoid cash payments. For example, an owner of a restaurant may give meals to an automobile mechanic in exchange for repairs; however, barter transactions are reportable for tax purposes based on the fair market value of what has been exchanged.

Payment to employees

Avoid giving employees cash advances such as funds for travel and entertainment or loans. You may delay the frequency of payments to employees (e.g., expense account reimbursements, payrolls). One way to do this is by having a monthly payroll rather than a weekly one. In this way, you can earn a return on the withheld monies.

Monitor payroll check-clearing dates. Salary checks are not all cashed on the payroll date, so funds can be deposited later and earn a return for you in the interim.

Disburse commissions on sales when receivables are collected rather than when the sales are made. Why pay a salesperson a commission on a sale that will not be collected for three months and may in fact never be collected at all? Further, if there is a collection problem with the account, your salesperson will be on the customer's "back" to pay so he/she will receive the commission.

Noncash compensation and remuneration methods may also be used with employees. Examples include giving employees stock or notes rather than immediate cash payment.

In many past recessions including the period 2008-2009, some employers eliminated or delayed payroll payments to employees. In some cases, employees were required to take furloughs (e.g., two weeks off without pay). In other cases, employees gave up current pay and agreed to be paid at a later date (e.g., postponing one week's pay to a later year or retirement).

You may also save money by hiring part-time employees since salaries are lower and fringe benefits typically are not given.

27 Are You Managing Debt Properly?

When you, as a business owner, buy on credit or take out loans, you have to be careful not to overextend yourself. Excessive debt means difficulties in paying interest and principal payments. If you are unable to make payments on time, you may have to refinance at higher interest rates, sell off key assets, or even default on the loans. Creditors can put you into bankruptcy! At the very least, your credit standing will suffer.

Here are some tips for managing debt:

- Avoid borrowing into the future to meet current business expenses. Are you borrowing against future sales revenue to pay for daily expenditures? If you are spending beyond your means, danger lurks ahead.
- Avoid borrowing for depreciating assets (those declining in value). Rather, borrow only for appreciating assets (those increasing in value).
- Always try to buy with cash rather than credit.
- Keep track of who is charging higher interest rates and move to a lower-cost source.
- Avoid using important assets as collateral, because you need them for ongoing business activities. Examples are inventory, company car, machinery, and office equipment.
- Avoid using high-cost debt financing because of the high interest charge. It is unwise to borrow and incur an 18 percent financing cost while putting money in the bank and earning only 6 percent. You should withdraw the savings and pay off the loan. Otherwise, you are losing 12 percent on your money.

- Avoid using borrowed funds to invest unless the interest rate on the loan is very low and there is a dependable investment return. Assume, for example, that you have $100,000 in a savings account earning 8 percent. You owe $70,000 on a loan at 20 percent interest. In this case, your net worth (assets less liabilities) is declining since the borrowing cost exceeds the return on the bank account by 12 percent. You should take $70,000 from the bank account to pay off the loan. Your reduction in net worth on an annual basis is:

Cost of loan ($70,000 x 20%)	$14,000
Return on bank account ($70,000 x 8%)	5,600
Decline in wealth	$ 8,400

- Establish a line of credit with the bank before you need it. There is usually no charge for a preapproved line until borrowing takes place.
- To reduce the dollar amount of each payment, extend loans over a longer time period (for example, financing the purchase of office equipment over five years rather than two years).

The advantages of buying assets or incurring expenses with debt are:

- *Convenience.* You do not have to pay by cash or give a check and can buy high-priced assets and pay them out.
- *Safety.* You do not need to carry lots of currency.
- *Ease of use in emergencies* when an unexpected expenditure occurs and you are temporarily out of cash.
- *Inflationary protection* because you can buy goods or services before large inflationary price increases occur.
- *Ease of returning merchandise* to suppliers since you have not paid for the item.
- *Avoidance of interest charges* (if you pay vendors within the credit-billing period).

The disadvantages of buying assets or incurring expenses with debt are:

- You can overextend by buying items or incurring expenditures you can not afford.
- You may be subject to high interest or other financing charges.
- You may end up feeling insecure. High debt may create insecurity and anxiety.
- If you do not pay on time, your credit rating may be adversely affected.

- You may tie up your funds in making debt payments so as to prevent you from making needed expenditures such as preventive maintenance and repairs.
- The debt may contain restrictive loan provisions such as a minimum working capital requirement. This will inhibit your freedom of action.

28 Collection Management

The small business owner should try to collect due payments as soon as possible to earn interest on the money. In addition, the longer it takes to collect, the greater the chance that the debt will end up uncollectible. Use good contact management software program, to track delinquent receivables, remind delinquent customers continually to pay, and note these danger signs of possible collection problems:

- Legal actions for collection against the customer by other suppliers
- The customer's failure to provide requested financial information.
- The customer's frequent changing of suppliers, banks, and other third parties.

Collection policy

You should mail customer statements on a regular basis (typically monthly). To save clerical costs, you may "cycle bill," mailing out statements throughout the month to balance the work schedule. For example, the first day of the month you may send out statements to customers with last names beginning with "A," while the last day of the month you may mail out statements to customers having a last name beginning with "Z." The customer's statement must contain the beginning balance, purchases, payments, dollar finance charge, annual percentage interest rate, ending balance, closing date of the statement, and the date the payment is due. Local laws may require that you have to wait at least 30 days after merchandise is sold before you can charge the customer interest on the amount of purchase.

If the customer uses a credit card (e.g., VISA, MasterCard), you will receive cash from the credit card issuer for the product or service before the customer remits payment to the credit card company. The advantage of accepting credit cards is that you generally avoid a collection problem since the credit card issuer is assuming the risk of collection. In addition, you have a better customer base because most consumers buy with credit cards; however, on the negative side, you must pay a fee to the credit card issuer based on the amount charged. Since there is a lot of record-keeping for charge purchases, you might tempt to establish a minimum charge amount (e.g., $10). According to the merchants' MasterCard and Visa contracts, you CANNOT require a minimum purchase. If you do, it violates their agreement with your bank issuer or credit card company.

Those charging with credit cards usually buy more and are less sensitive to the selling price; however, if you unknowingly accept a stolen or counterfeited credit card, you are responsible. A customer may also refuse to pay the credit card issuer for a disputed item, in which case, you may be charged back the amount by the credit card company. Further, credit card holders are more likely to return merchandise than are customers who pay cash.

In selling seasonal merchandise, you may offer an installment plan in which you agree to receive remissions over many months. The installment arrangement is more suitable for expensive goods, usually durable items (e.g., furniture, appliances) that have high value and longevity. The merchandise may be repossessed if the customer misses a payment. A higher down payment (e.g., 30%) is beneficial because it makes the consumer feel like an owner and, if coupled with higher monthly payments, provides you protection from a decline in the value of the merchandise if it becomes necessary to repossess. It is best when the unpaid balance is less than the market value of the item since that provides motivation for the consumer to want to keep it; if it is the other way around, the consumer will not care to keep property that is worth less than what is owed on a loan.

In setting a collection policy, it is wise to follow these practices:

- Requesting earlier payment from customers currently experiencing financial difficulties. Further, withhold additional products or services until payment is made.
- Bill for large sales immediately.
- Bill for services as performed or receive an advance payment (e.g., a retainer paid to an accountant or attorney).
- Invoice customers for merchandise when the order is processed instead of when it is shipped.
- Offer a price discount if the customer pays for the goods before delivery.
- Age the accounts receivable to identify delinquent accounts; that is, determine the number of days individual customer balances have been uncollected. The longer the customer's balance remains open, the greater the risk you will not collect the account. Interest should be charged on delinquent accounts.
- Factor (sell) accounts receivable when net savings arise; however, be aware that confidential information may be disclosed. Some of the author's clients

are reluctant to factor receivables because they fear that a competitive retailer may in some way obtain useful information.

- Monitor customer complaints about order item and invoice errors and orders not filled on time.

Use the following system to collect on delinquent accounts:

- *Start the follow-up process early.* Contact problem accounts within three to five days of their becoming overdue. Waiting 60 or 90 days not only puts a major dent in your cash flow, it puts delinquent customers in an embarrassing situation because they know they are overdue. Often, rather than square the account, they put your receivables at the bottom of their payables pile and take their business to a competitor. To justify their actions, they may start bad-mouthing your company or complain about nonexistent problems with your product or service.
- *Call the largest accounts first.* Most companies call their delinquent accounts in alphabetical order. Instead, forego that approach and go after the customers that owe you the big bucks. Why? Because 20% of your accounts usually represent 80% of the dollars. Do your cash flow a favor by starting with the largest accounts and working your way down to the smaller ones.
- *Keep a log to track systems problems.* Customers often become delinquent because of billing or invoicing errors on your part. By tracking your accounts-receivable systems problems and your solutions to those problems, you can respond to billing glitches in a timely and efficient manner, thereby eliminating a common excuse for late payments. A good tracking system also allows you to upgrade your business processes continually and provide better service to your customers.
- *Call at the right time.* The best time to call commercial accounts is Monday morning. Start calling personal customers Thursday and go through Friday, when people usually get paid.

Offering a discount

Should you offer a discount to customers if they pay their accounts early? The answer is yes if the return on the money received earlier exceeds the cost of the discount.

For example, assume that your current annual credit sales are $1.2 million. You sell on terms of net/30, and your collection period is two months. Therefore, the turnover of accounts receivable is six times (12/2). You expect a 15% rate of return. You propose to offer a 3/10, net/30 discount. You anticipate 20% of your customers will take advantage of the discount. The discount policy is expected to reduce the collection period to 1 ½ months (turnover of eight times). The discount policy should be instituted as indicated below.

Current average accounts receivable balance ($1,200,000/6)		$200,000
Average accounts receivable balance after change in policy ($1,200,000/8)		150,000
Reduction in average accounts receivable		$ 50,000
Rate of return	x .15	
Dollar return earned		$ 7,500
Cost of discount (0.20 x $1,200,000 x .03)		7,200
Advantage of discount policy		$ 300

Collection agency

You should transfer a delinquent account to a collection agency six months from the time goods were bought; however, collection agencies charge a significant fee. You may sue a delinquent customer to receive payment. If not much money is involved, you may take the customer to small claims court; the advantage with this is that you do not need an attorney; however, you should go to court only when the probability of collection is high and the amount warrants it. There are disadvantages to taking legal action, including court costs, time, and aggravation.

29 Credit Management

Retailers usually extend less credit than manufacturers and wholesalers because individual consumers present a higher risk of uncollectibility than do corporate accounts.

In extending credit to retail customers, you should consider both the amount and the terms, which will influence your sales and the resulting profitability, the collection period, and the number of delinquent or uncollectible accounts. If you establish stringent credit terms, you will have lower sales revenue and net income, less money tied up in customer balances, lower bad-debt losses, and adverse customer reaction. If your credit policy is too lax, you will experience higher sales, higher accounts receivable balances, and more bad debts.

Should you liberalize credit?

In deciding whether to offer liberal credit terms and thus sell to more risky customers, you have to compare the profitability on the additional sales to the increased uncollectible accounts, higher investing and collection costs, and the return you lose by tying up money in accounts receivable for a longer time period. The investment in accounts receivable may be computed by multiplying the annual credit sales by the ratio of the days receivables are held to 360 days in a year.

Suppose, for example, that you sell on terms of net/30. The customer accounts are on average 20 days past due. Annual credit sales are $60,000. The average investment in accounts receivable is;

$$\frac{50}{360} \text{ x } \$600{,}000 = \$83{,}333$$

Receivable terms should be liberalized when you want to dispose of excessive inventory or obsolete items. Longer receivable terms are appropriate for retailers whose products are sold in advance of "demand" seasons (e.g., swimsuits). If products are perishable, short credit terms or even payment on delivery is recommended.

You may have to alter your credit policy based on changing situations and circumstances. When times are good, you may grant additional credit. However, when times are bad, it's smart to tighten up on granting credit, because higher unemployment rates, salary freezes, and employee givebacks reduce customers' ability to pay their bills. The amount of credit you can safely extend also depends on competitive factors and the incomes of your customers.

Credit policy also varies with the type of business. A vegetable or fruit store will most likely sell only on a cash basis because of the perishability of the product. An appliance store will likely include sales on the *installment payment basis* because of the long life of its product line. A service business may ask for advance payments (retainers) or may bill clients when services are performed.

Evaluating a customer's credit

In evaluating a prospective customer's ability to pay, you should take into account previous experience with that customer, the customer's honesty, and the customer's financial health, including assets and income. If you expect a possible collection problem or the economic environment is unfavorable, you may insist upon receiving collateral.

In all cases, check customer references by calling the customer's bank, employer, insurance company, and other retailers. A salesperson's opinion should not necessarily be relied upon because the salesperson wants to make a commission and is not an expert in evaluating credit soundness. In any event, you should charge back to the salesperson the commission paid when an account becomes uncollectible.

Sources of credit information

There are a number of sources you may refer to in obtaining credit information about corporate or individual customers. They include:

- *Suppliers*. The people you buy from may have previously sold to or may be currently selling to those who are now asking you for credit.
- *Credit Bureaus*. These organizations are in the business of furnishing credit reports on business firms and individuals. In selecting a particular credit bureau, consider its reputation, coverage, accuracy, timeliness, and fee. Examples are Trans Union - PO Box 390, Springfield, PA, (800) 916-8800, Esperian (P.O. Box 949, Allen, TX 75002, (800) 682-7654), and Equifax (P.O. Box 105873 Atlanta, GA 30348, (800) 685-1111). You may obtain credit information and reports in computerized form instantly by accessing through your personal computer and telecommunications software an on-line data base of credit information.

- *Mercantile Credit Agencies*. These organizations will provide you with their analysis of the financial standing of a potential corporate customer for a fee. When a prospective customer contacts you, have him or her complete a credit application form. The form should require answers to questions such as the name of the employer and how many years the applicant has worked there, type of position, salary, other sources of income, bank accounts, total assets, total owed, and insurance policies.

Credit policy

Your credit policy should be flexible and tied into the peculiar characteristics of the customer (e.g., age, occupation, income), merchandise or services offered, selling price, cost of the item, profit margin (profit divided by selling price), goals of the business, cash position, liquidity, degree of competition, and shipping arrangements. In deciding upon a credit policy, the following should be taken into account:

- *Marketing aspects of the product line.* For example, if your credit terms are too tight, the customer may go elsewhere and you will have lost a sale.
- *Financial condition of the customer.* As this changes, so should the credit limit. For example, a customer who loses his or her job should receive restricted or no credit.
- *Seasonal fluctuations.* If you have a policy of seasonal datings (billing at the end of a season), you may provide liberal terms when business is slow to stimulate sales by selling to those who cannot pay now but will have money later in the season, such as an employee (e.g., stockbroker, executive) who may be short of money in September but who will have a lot of money in December when he or she receives a year-end bonus. This policy is justifiable when the profit on the additional sales plus the decreased costs of storing inventory exceeds the return lost from holding receivable balances for a longer period of time.

The Truth-in-Lending Law passed by the U.S. government requires that credit agreements include the selling price of goods or services, the down payment, the amount to be financed, the interest and financing charges and how they are computed, the annual interest rate, the number and amount of payments, the principal and interest portions of each payment, the due date of payments, penalty charges, and the nature and amount of collateral required.

There is a greater default risk from consumer receivables than corporate receivables, and smaller companies are less likely to pay than larger companies.

Try to avoid typically high-risk receivables (e.g., individuals in a depressed locality, companies in financially troubled industries). Be wary of small corporate accounts in business less than two years since the probability of failure for such ventures is high.

Consider credit insurance to guard against unusual bad debt losses. In deciding whether to obtain such insurance, take into account expected losses, your financial ability to withstand the losses, and the cost of the insurance.

FICO scores

A FICO (an acronym for Fair, Isaac & Company), or credit score is a computer-generated numerical grade that predicts a lender's risk in doing business with a borrower. Any company or individual that issues mortgage loans, home-equity loans, car loans, insurance policies, or healthcare services (even the IRS) bases much of its lending decisions and terms on the applicant's FICO score. FICO scores are determined by computers and released through the three credit bureaus to their subscribing members. At Experian. the scores are called *Experian/Fair, Isaac*; at Equifax, they are called *Beacon* scores; at Trans Union, they are called *Empirica* scores.

Scoring is based on things like time on the job, the time you've lived at your current address, plus about 30 other factors, none of which are your income or assets:

1. *Payment history.* Do you make your payments on time? Have you had accounts turned over to collection? FICO deducts points for bad behavior, and it gives points for maintaining a good payment relationship.
2. *Outstanding debt.* FICO is very interested in the number of balances you have currently; the average of all balances, and the relationship between the total balance and total credit limit. Carrying too much credit lowers your score even if some of your accounts have zero balances, but FICO doesn't like to see you close to or at your limits, either.
3. *Credit history.* FICO looks at how long you've had those accounts, the total number of inquiries, and if you have opened new accounts. It is highly concerned about inquiries and accounts less than 12 months old.
4. *The types of credit you use.* FICO is very interested in the diversity of the credit you use. It looks to see if you use department store or bankcards, debit or credit cards, travel and entertainment cards, personal finance companies, and installment loans.
5. *Negative information.* Bankruptcies, late payments, collections, late fees, too many credit lines with maximum available funds borrowed, too little credit history (less than five credit lines in the past two years), and too many credit report inquiries are considered negatives.

What is considered a good score varies from lender to lender. FICO scores range from 375 to 900 points, and a score of 650 to 675 is generally considered excellent; however, to qualify for the most favorable terms, a lender might require a score in excess of 700.

MODULE 8

Smart Banking

30 Preparing a Bank Reconciliation

Small businesses receive monthly bank statements showing deposits made, checks cleared, various charges (deductions) and credits (additions), and the bank account balances at the beginning and end of the period.

As you know, the ending balance in the bank statement rarely agrees with the ending balance in your checkbook (book balance). To resolve the discrepancy, you should perform a *bank reconciliation*. Once completed, the *adjusted bank balance* must match the *adjusted checkbook balance*. When it does, both records are correct.

The bank balance is adjusted for items reflected on your records that are *not* on the bank statement. They include:

- *Outstanding checks.* These are checks that you issued but that have not yet cleared the bank. The total of the outstanding checks is deducted from the bank balance. The exception is an uncleared certified check, which is not considered outstanding since both parties-you and the bank-know about it. A certified check is one for which the bank immediately sets aside funds for payment when the check is presented for certification.
- *Deposits in transit.* This refers to cash or checks you received at the end of the period that have not been deposited or were deposited after the bank prepared it's' statement. Such deposits are added to the bank balance.
- *Errors in recording checks.* Mistakes, such as transposition errors, can be made in the recording of checks. For example, an item should be adjusted on the bank balance if it was previously overstated on your checkbook.
- *Bank errors in charging or crediting your account.* If your account is charged in error for another company's check, your bank balance is understated. Add the amount of the check to your bank balance. On the other hand,

if a deposit made by another is incorrectly credited to your account, you should reduce the bank balance. Of course, contact your bank to discuss the errors.

Your checkbook balance is also adjusted for items shown on the bank statement that are not reflected on your records. These include:

- *Bank charges.* Fees for bank services are a reduction of your checkbook balance. These amounts are not known until the bank statement is received. Examples include the monthly service charge, cost per check, check printing costs, and stop-payment fees.
- *NSF (Not Sufficient Funds) checks.* These are checks that have bounced because of insufficient funds in your customer's checking account. In this case, the bank issues a debit memorandum for the dishonored amount and hence your checkbook balance is reduced.
- *Collections.* Notes and other items are collected by the bank for a nominal fee. The proceeds received less the charge (in the form of a credit memorandum) are credited to your account. The net amount acts as an addition to the book balance. Examples are a note a customer gave you and a check received from an international customer who ordered your merchandise. The latter requires the bank to determine the proper exchange rate to use on the date the check is cashed.
- *Interest earned.* Interest income credited by the bank on the checking account increases the book balance.
- *Error on the books.* Various types of mistakes can be made on your books. Two examples and explanations of how they can be corrected follow.

  (Assume the amount of the check is correct.) Assume a check is written ($50) for more than the amount entered as a cash payment ($45) in your checkbook. In this case, your cash disbursements are understated by $5 and the balance per your checkbook should be reduced by that amount.

  A check is written ($100) for less than the amount shown as a cash payment ($120) in your checkbook. Here, cash payments are overstated. The checkbook balance should be increased by $20 to correct for the error.

The following example involves a bank reconciliation. On June 30, 2x10, Quick Retail Store prepares a bank reconciliation. The balance on the bank statement is $4,889, while the checkbook balance shows $4,400. Outstanding checks are #410, for $500, and #423, for $200. A deposit of $300 was made in the night depository at the bank. There was a collection on a note of $216 less a collection fee of $12. Bill Clone's check for $100 did *not* clear. The bank's monthly service fee was $15.

Balance per bank		$4,889
Add: Deposit in transit		300
		$5,189
Less: Outstanding checks		
#410	$500	
#423	200	700
Adjusted bank balance		$4,489
Balance per books		$4,400
Add: Proceeds on note		216
		$4,616
Less: NSF check	$100	
Collection fee	12	
Service charge	15	127
Adjusted book balance		$4,489

31 Float

It is in your best interest to receive payments from your customers as quickly as possible and to make payments to your creditors as slowly as possible so that you can invest the funds and maximize your investment return. When you receive checks from your customers, deposit them immediately. This allows you to have use of the funds as soon as the checks clear and minimizes the possibility that the check will be returned for insufficient funds (if your suspect the payor is in financial difficulty, it's best to make your claim against any available funds as quickly as possible). Similarly, it's smart to delay payments to your creditors for as long as possible so that you can retain use of the money until the last minute.

Float is defined as the difference between the cash balance your records show and the cash balance the bank's records show. Float results from writing checks that have not yet cleared (disbursement float) and from customer checks that have been received but not yet cleared (called collection float). Float makes it possible for your bank book balance to be negative while the bank shows your balance as being positive.

There are several types of delays in processing checks:

1. *Mail float;* the time required for a check to move from someone to you.
2. *Processing float;* the time needed for you to enter the payment in your records.
3. *Deposit collection float;* the time for a check to clear.

Determine the causes for delays in depositing cash receipts and take corrective action. Ascertain *how* and *where* the cash receipts come, how cash is transferred to your bank account, the bank's policy regarding availability of funds, and the length of time between when a check is received and when it is deposited. You want money available to you as soon as possible so you can earn interest.

Fig. 31-1 is a schematic float calendar for a small business.

It is also important to consider *lost float*. For example, 2 days float on $200,000 at a 10% interest rate costs you:

$111 ($200,000 x 10% x 2/360).

The acceleration of cash inflow enables you to profit through reduced float. If deposits average $20,000 per day and the mailing and collection time can be reduced by three days, your business will have $60,000 in additional usable funds. Assuming a rate of return of 10%, the value of those funds is $6,000 per year in savings.

If float is used effectively, you may get an "interest-free" loan from the bank. For example, assume you have a $5,000 balance in your checking account (noninterest-bearing) and $150,000 in your money market account. You write a check for $20,000, which you expect to clear in five days. On the fifth day, you transfer $15,000 from the savings account to the checking account to cover the check. You have successfully used five days' float to earn interest on the $15,000 for five days. The check will clear because your checking account balance is $20,000 ($15,000 + $5,000).

The amount of float depends on both (1) the *time lag* and (2) the *dollars involved.* Float may be determined in dollar-days, multiplying the lag in days by the dollar amount delayed. The *cost* of float is the interest lost because the money was not available for investment or the interest paid because money had to be borrowed during the lag period. The cost of float is computed by multiplying the average daily float by the cost of capital (opportunity cost) for the time period under consideration. Consider the following example.

ITEM	DOLLAR AMOUNT		NUMBER OF DAYS		DOLLAR DAYS
1	$20,000	X	3	=	$60,000
2	10,000	X	2	=	20,000
3	30,000	X	4	=	120,000
	$60,000				$200,000

Average daily float = $200,000/30 days = $6,667

Average daily receipts = $60,000/30 days = $2,000

Average daily days = $200,000/$60,000 = 3.333 days

Average daily float = $2,000 x 3.3333 = $6,667

Average cost of float = $6,667 x .09 (the cost of capital assumed) = $600

Note: Electronic data exchange (EDI) or financial EDI (FEDI) significantly reduces or eliminates a float. EDI refers to the growing practice of direct, electronic information exchange between all types of businesses, thereby shortening the length of time required to initiate and complete a business transaction.

Figure 31.1: Schematic Float Calendar

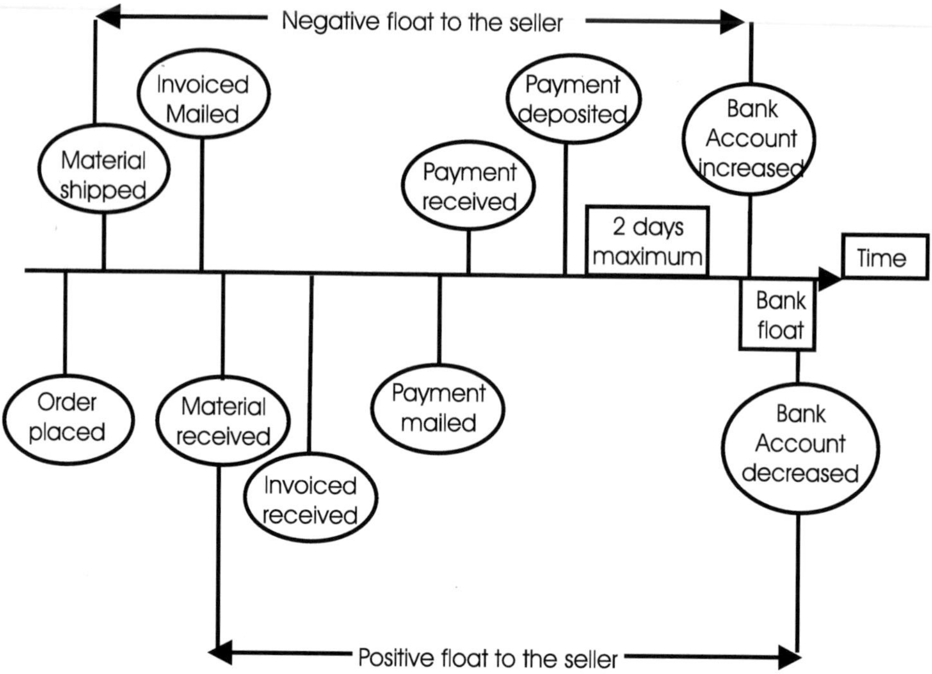

32 Electronic Funds Transfer (EFT)

Electronic funds transfer, commonly known as EFT, refers to a number of systems linked electronically via a communications network—telephone, computer terminal, or microcomputer.

With EFT, a fund transfer is charged to the payor's bank account the same day it is credited to the payee's bank account. As a result, payment float disappears and funds are instantly available.

EFT speeds customer collections because funds are automatically transferred to your bank account from your customer's account on the due date. An EFT may be used for either constant or variable payments. Collection problems are fewer from unpaid bills and cancellations of discretionary payments, and customers find paying by home computer convenient.

EFT may be used for the following:

- Transferring funds between bank accounts, such as from an interest-bearing savings account to a noninterest bearing checking account.
- Making automatic payments for suppliers and for operating expenses at regular intervals.
- Receiving funds to be deposited into an account.
- Obtaining up-to-date account information.
- Making direct deposits of payroll to employee bank accounts.

Cash planning is enhanced through EFT because you can predict with more accuracy when cash will be received and when disbursement will be made. This provides a good indicator of what your cash balance will be on a given day.

By joining an EFT system, you enjoy the following benefits:

- Lower costs for making payments and receiving collections.
- Lower bank charges because of reduced check volume and fewer bank accounts because of fast electronic transmission.
- Lower bookkeeping costs.
- Immediate availability of funds without having to wait for checks to clear.
- Paperless transactions, improving both speed and accuracy of transactions.
- Fewer lost or stolen receipts or payments.
- Better use of employee time.
- Enhanced internal control over cash.
- Accurate accounts of transactions.
- Better service to employees and retirees; makes funds available to them sooner without the danger of checks getting lost in the mail or the inconvenience of having to deposit checks.
- Better control over the timing of the payment process.
- Enhanced investment planning ability.
- Improved cash flow forecasting accuracy.
- Easy use of customer credit cards that are automatically validated at your retail store, charging the buyer's account electronically.
- Access to wire transfers between banks and other financial institutions (see next section).

Wire transfers

To speed up the receipt of cash, you may *wire transfer* funds between banks. Wire transfers are recommended primarily when there are high dollar amounts involved, because both the originating and the receiving banks usually charge high per-wire transfer fees. Examples of wire transfers include making transfers for investment purposes, transferring funds to a checking account at the time checks are going to clear, and placing funds in any other accounts that need those funds. With wire transfers (e.g., bank wire, Federal Reserve wire), funds are moved immediately between banks. This eliminates transit float in that only "good funds" are transferred.

Wire transfers may be either recurring (preformatted) or nonrepetitive (free-form). *Recurring transfers* are appropriate for frequent, predictable transfers. You specify the issuing and receiving banks and the account number. *Nonrecurring transfers* are of varying amounts and are made at different times. Since a great degree of control is needed for wire transfers, it is best to act only after receiving written confirmation, not oral ones. The account may be funded on a staggered basis to maintain control over balances. To guard against an overdraft, there should be sufficient balances on deposit in other accounts.

Internal controls should be established over electronic fund transfers to guard against unauthorized transactions.

Examples of controls over wire transfers are the use of passwords and prohibited use during nonworking hours.

33 Utilizing a Lockbox

If your business receives many checks from customers, time and money are devoted to processing these deposits and waiting for checks to clear. A lockbox arrangement may be appropriate. Further, a business with a large volume of customer remittances by mail could most likely reduce the risk of employee misappropriation of cash by using this arrangement.

A *lockbox* is one in which the best collection point (such as a post office box or private mail box) is placed near customers. Customer payments are mailed to strategic post office boxes geographically situated in local areas to hasten mailing and depositing time. Banks or third parties collect from these boxes several times a day and make deposits to your account. There may be a special ZIP code assigned for remittances by the bank. A lockbox arrangement is cost-effective when there are many checks of higher dollar amounts involved to justify processing charges.

The bank remits to the company a list of checks received by account number, a daily total, and any notes from customers. In addition, there is a return document in paper or card form that is read by an optimal character recognition device. This gives you earlier notification of bad checks. A lockbox arrangement also simplifies the record-keeping process.

To help determine whether you should use a lockbox, calculate the average dollar amount of checks received, the cost of clerical operations that would be eliminated, and the reduction in "mail float" days. Because per-time processing costs are usually significant, it is most advantageous to use a lockbox with low-volume, high-dollar collections. The system is becoming available to small businesses with high-volume, low-dollar receipts as technological advances lower the per-item cost of lockboxes.

A *wholesale lockbox* is used for checks receipted from other companies when the average dollar of cash receipts is large and the number of cash receipts is small. The bank prepares an electronic list of receipts and transmits the information to you. Many wholesale lockboxes result in mail-time reductions of no more than one business day and check-clearing time reductions of only a few tenths of one day. Wholesale lockboxes are beneficial if you have annual gross revenues of a few million dollars and if you receive large checks from distant customers, as you would if your business handles mail-order sales.

A *retail lockbox* is best if you deal with the public (retail consumers). Retail lockboxes typically have many transactions involving nominal amounts. The lockbox reduces float and transfers workload from your business to the bank. The net effect is improved cash flow and reduced expenses.

For example, if it takes about eight days to receive and deposit payments from customers, a lockbox arrangement may reduce the float time to five days. Also assume average daily collections are $40,000 and the return rate is 12%.

If the lockbox system is initiated, the decline in outstanding cash balances would be the following:

Three days X $40,000 = $120,000

The annual return that could be earned on these funds is

$120,000 X .12 = $14,400

The maximum monthly charge that should be paid for the lockbox system is

$14,400/12 = $1,200

As another example, perhaps you are thinking of using a lockbox system costing $15,000 per year. Daily collections average $36,000. The lockbox arrangement will reduce the float period by four days. The rate of return is 13%.

The cost-benefit analysis is shown as follows:

Return on early collection of cash	
(.13 x 4 x $36,000)	$18,720
Less: Cost	15,000
Advantage of lockbox	$ 3,720

As a final example, you have an agreement with ABC Bank which handles $40,000 in collections a day and requires a compensating balance of $6,000. You are considering canceling the agreement and dividing the western region using XYZ Bank to handle $10,000 a day in collections and a compensating balance of $2,000 and DEF Bank to handle the other $30,000 a day in collections and a compensating balance of $5,000. It is expected that collections will be hastened by ¼ day if you divide the western region. The rate of return is 12%.

Acceleration in cash receipts (40,000 x ¼)	$10,000
Less: Additional compensating balance ($7,000-$6,000)	1,000
Increased cash flow	$ 9,000
Times: Rate of return	x .12
Net annual savings	$ 1,080

34 Depository Transfer Checks and Pre-authorized Debits (PADs)

A small business with a few stores may wish to consolidate the money deposited to its accounts at different locations into a central account to speed up cash receipts. In a *deposit transfer check* arrangement, funds deposited into local bank accounts at various locations are automatically transferred into a central account. "Cash concentration" results in better control and use of funds.

Depository transfer checks (DTCs) are checks used to transfer money between bank accounts. A signature is not needed on DTCs. The check (which can be paper or paperless) is payable to the bank but is credited to your account. Manual DTCs are preprinted checks that contain all relevant information except for the date and amount. Automated DTCs are printed when needed. It is cheaper to use the bank's printer than to buy your own checks elsewhere. Automatic check preparation is recommended when many transfer checks are used each day.

You may receive cash faster from customers if you have obtained permission to charge their accounts routinely and automatically. This is called *preauthorized debits* (PADs). An insurance broker, for example, may charge semiannual PADs to client accounts. PADs save you the costs of sending invoices to customers, receiving remittances through the mail, processing payments, and depositing checks.

PADs are better for handling *fixed* payments than *variable* payments. Since the latter by definition change each time, the customer must be notified of the amount to be charged beforehand and must approve it. The use of PADs work well for repeated, constant charges at given time intervals (monthly, bi-monthly, quarterly). Preauthorized checks are the most common form of such charges.

Through the use of debit cards at an automatic teller machine (ATM), customers can transfer funds electronically from their accounts to the account of the small business.

Internal controls are needed when using debit cards because of possible theft of funds. Make sure identification information is difficult for someone to obtain.

For example, it is easier for a thief to obtain your social security number than your mother's maiden name.

35 Cost-Benefit Analysis of Cash Management Devices

Cost-benefit analysis can help you decide whether a particular collection or disbursement service will save you money. The use of a particular service is justified as long as the added benefit exceeds the added costs, yielding a net benefit. Of course, if you consider two alternative systems, you choose the one resulting in higher profitability.

The lockbox system (discussed in Key 33) generates more benefits-in the form of cost savings because of a lower float (discussed in Key 31)-than does the *field collection system* (remittances sent to geographically situated offices), since the operating bank is more efficient and the configuration of cities used is better; however, the lockbox system is more costly to operate.

Here's an example: TLC Company is comparing the costs and benefits of setting up a lockbox system and a field collection system to replace the present cash receipt arrangement, which uses neither. The following data are available:

Interest rate: 10%

Lockbox system

The lockbox system would free up an additional annual average of $60,000 float over the current arrangement. The increase in costs would total $4,000 per year.

Field collection system

This would free up an additional annual average of $40,000 float over the current arrangement. The increase in costs would total $3,000 per year. Calculate the net savings of both systems as follows:

	LOCK BOX SYSTEM	*FIELD COLLECTION SYSTEM*
Added benefit	10% ($60,000) = $6,000 per year	10% (40,000) = $4,000 per year
Added cost	4,000	3,000
Net savings	$2,000	$1,000

While both systems offer improvements over the current system, the lockbox arrangement is the better of the two.

There are other ways to accelerate cash collections such as billing early, coded return envelopes, electronic transfers, cash on delivery, and advance payment. See Key 28.

MODULE 9

Obtaining Cash and Borrowing

36 Improving Personal Cash Receipts

There are several ways in which you, as a business owner, can obtain money sooner to either invest it for a return, pay bills, or reduce debt.

When you apply for insurance reimbursement in connection with medical and dental coverage or for losses incurred, such as those involving auto accidents and theft, file your insurance reimbursement application early to obtain the funds. For example, if you file your application on the date you incur the expenditure (e.g., payment to the doctor on January 10), you have the use of the reimbursed money sooner than if you filed the application for all physician charges at the end of the year (e.g., December 31).

Have deposits automatically credited to your bank account so you earn interest on the money sooner. For example, social security checks and salaries may be transferred directly to your account. When you retire, you may elect to receive the accumulated retirement funds in one lump sum rather than being paid in an annuity over time.

When the Internal Revenue Service or a state owes you a tax refund, file as early as possible to receive that refund. Why wait to file on the April 15 due date if you can receive that refund early and deposit it in your bank account to earn interest?

If you need money, sell your stock or bond investments now rather than holding on to them. The cost of borrowing typically exceeds the rate of return on investments.

In a divorce settlement, arrange to have your ex-spouse pay you higher alimony payments in the earlier years since cash received earlier is worth more than cash received later because of inflation. You are better off receiving child support payments rather than alimony because the formers are not taxable to you.

If you are a landlord, make sure the tenant pays you at the beginning of the month rather than at the end. Also, get a security deposit.

If you receive royalty income, try to get a significant royalty advance. For example, if you are an author of a book, try to contract for a high royalty advance before the book is published.

If you are a salesperson receiving commissions after your company receives collection from the customer, ask to be paid the commission once the sale is made because you have already expended the effort, rather than when the customer pays for the merchandise.

To receive cash sooner, you may request your employer to pay you more often. For example, if you are currently being paid monthly, you may be able to convince your employer to pay you bi-weekly.

37 Financing Cash Requirement

Cash from operations is the best source of funds for meeting your business's liquidity needs, since it represents internally generated cash derived from net income from the basic operating activities of the business. However, there are a number of ways to obtain additional funds for liquidity when your cash balance and marketable securities are inadequate to meet the needs of your business. This Key discusses several options.

The diagram below shows that money for future cash payments may be obtained from future cash inflows, the existing cash balance, sale of marketable securities, or short-term borrowing.

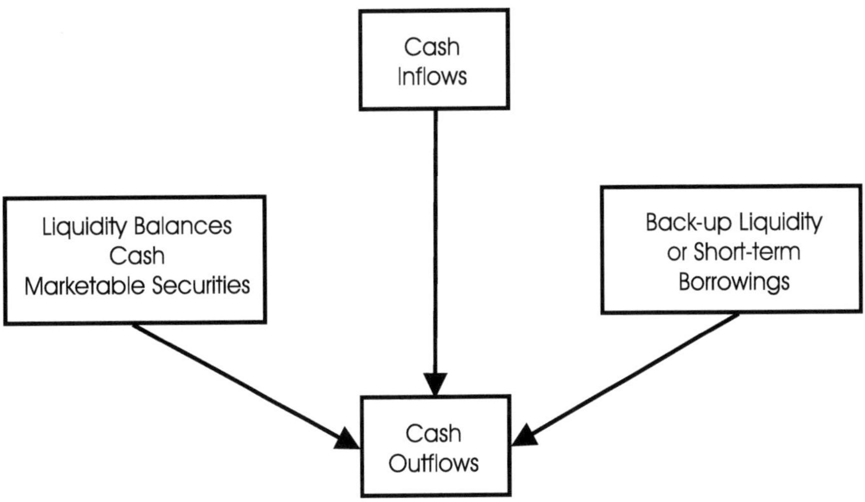

In selecting a particular way to finance, you should consider:

- *Cost.* The financing cost should be within reason.
- *Timing.* The timing of the payments should be such that you can easily make payments when due.

- *Availability.* The financing source should be available when you need it in the future.
- *Interference.* The lender or investor may want to interfere in your business or obtain some degree of control. Try to minimize this.
- *Risk.* The risk applicable to a financing source must be evaluated. For example, taking out a loan requiring substantial initial monthly payments is more risky than a loan in which the payments are equal each month.
- *Restrictions.* Try to avoid loans that place restrictions on the business or inhibit your managerial freedom. For example, a bank may stipulate that you cannot use money for a particular purpose.
- *Partnership.* One important means of obtaining cash is bringing in one or more partners who make a capital contribution; however, a partnership has several drawbacks: you have to share profits; you are legally liable for the actions of your partner; and the partnership has a limited life because it ends when either partner dies.
- *Borrowing.* Your ability to borrow on a short-term basis may be referred to as back-up liquidity (see diagram page 86). In taking out debt, there are many considerations.

You may use the hedging technique, financing business assets with debt of the same maturity so the monies obtained from the return on, and selling price of, the assets are enough to pay the debt when due. It is dangerous to buy 10-year equipment with a six-month loan because the loan will have to be paid well before sufficient cash is received from the asset.

Debt financing is an easy and fast method to obtain money. The loan is typically tied into a particular business purpose; however, lenders are very cautious when lending to a new small business because of the high probability of failure. The interest rate charged will be higher and collateral will be required to compensate for the perceived greater risk of the business.

In deciding on a debt repayment schedule, avoid due dates shortly after year-end when cash might be tight. This allows funds to be used for other operating purposes. Further, payments should be scheduled to be made on a day when cash surpluses are anticipated. When possible, cash receipts should be obtained before cash payments are made.

Equipment may serve as collateral for a loan, often up to 75% of its fair market value. The loan payment period is typically related to the equipment's expected life.

Real estate may serve as security for a loan; you can even use your home as equity. Mortgages may be obtained for about 75% of the fair market value of the property and allow payments to be made over the long term (e.g., 25 years), enabling you to retain funds to meet short-term cash needs.

Issuing stock

In an incorporated small business, funds may be obtained from the issuance of stock, giving an equity interest in the business to a third party. Stock issues require no repayment in the form of principal and interest; therefore, the cash received does not have to be paid back. Further, since stock financing increases equity, it improves the credit rating of the business compared to debt financing. On the negative side, stock issuance gives up part of the ownership in a business and permits others to enjoy the appreciation in value of the business. Stockholders are not personally liable for the unpaid obligations of a bankrupt company.

The disadvantages of issuing stock are:

- The cost of stock issuance exceeds that of debt.
- Dividend payments are not tax deductible.
- Ownership interest is diluted.
- Voting control is partly given up.

Venture capital

When financing a recently started small business with a high degree of risk, you may seek venture capital. Due to the perceived risk, your business will be analyzed and examined quite prudently and stringently by the venture capitalist. In most cases, venture capitalists will demand a substantial stake in the business; however, they usually allow you to run the business on a daily basis as you see fit. Venture capitalists typically demand a high return for the risk they are assuming.

A "finder" may arrange for financing your small business. A finder receives a percentage commission based on how much money is obtained. For example, if a finder raises $150,000 and he or she charges 10%, the finder's fee is $15,000. You may refer to financial magazines and newspaper for the names of finders.

The small business owner must assure himself that he is not overburdened with excessive debt. This is an especially acute problem in recessionary times.

The trend in the ratio of debt to equity should be examined over time and relative to other small businesses.

38 Marketable Securities and Money Market Funds

Marketable securities are readily tradable securities with short-term maturities (i.e., one year or less). The management of marketable securities is a major aspect of cash management. Some small businesses have a marketable security portfolio in excess of their cash balance. The objectives of investing in marketable securities are to:

1. Ensure cash is immediately available.
2. Ensure the safety of principal.
3. Minimize the risk of loss.

Examples of these liquid securities are:

- *U.S. Treasury bills*—highly liquid (marketable) instruments having a maturity ranging from 90 days to one year, guaranteed by the U.S. government. The minimum denomination is $10,000. Treasuries are issued on a discount basis, meaning that you pay less than face value but receive the face amount at maturity. The difference represents the interest earned. For example, you might buy a six-month treasury-commonly referred to as a T-bill-for $9,700 but receive $10,000 at maturity. You have earned $300 in interest. U.S. Treasury securities can be bought directly through the Federal Reserve System or from a broker.
- *U.S. Treasury notes and bonds*—obligations of the U.S. government having a maturity ranging from one year to 30 years. They are typically issued in minimum denominations of $1,000.

- *Commercial paper*—short-term, unsecured promissory notes issued by financially strong companies, they are in effect corporate IOUs. The maturity date is usually less than 270 days, and the minimum denomination is typically from $25,000 to $100,000. These are also issued on a discount basis. The interest rate is about three-quarters of a percent higher than that for comparable Treasury bills.
- *Certificate of deposit*—short-term, negotiable time deposits with banks issued at face value and providing for interest either at maturity or periodically (e.g., monthly); the bank promises to pay the amount deposited plus interest on the date specified. They are temporary investments rather than cash because they cannot be immediately withdrawn. The maturity period varies from 30 days to several years. Interest rates on certificates of deposit are about one-half point higher than that on comparable U.S. government issuances.
- *Money market funds*—managed portfolios of short-term debt instruments such as Treasury bills and commercial paper. They usually have a high degree of safety and liquidity.

A small business with an investment portfolio of $100,000 or less and limited cash availability should invest only in Treasury bills. On the other hand, a small business with more than $100,000 in its investment portfolio may utilize higher risk investments to maximize its rate of return.

The investment period should match the time when the cash will be needed. For example, if money will be needed to pay bills in three months, a three-month certificate of deposit should be selected.

Temporary excess cash, usually arising in slow operating periods, may be invested in marketable securities for a return; however, the return on marketable securities is usually much less than the return on operating assets. A seasonal business may buy marketable securities when it has surplus funds and then sell the securities when cash deficits occur. Also, holding marketable securities serves as protection against cash shortages that may occur during peak operating periods. Funds may also be held *temporarily* in marketable securities in the following cases:

1. in expectation of short-term expansion by buying assets,
2. for payment of future operating expenses,
3. for payment of obligations at a future date.

In times of recession, more cash should be held and any investments should be in safe marketable securities. Furthermore, a seasonal, risky small business should seek safe investments. A small business that requires a cash cushion against an unexpected eventuality should invest in high-quality short-term securities; however, a secure small business with stable sales may take greater risk.

A conservative policy is to invest in marketable securities only during slow seasons. A more aggressive strategy is to hold some marketable securities and concurrently seek short-term loans during peak operating periods.

In managing your investments, you must establish

1. your investment objectives
2. your criteria for selecting investments
3. the timing of changes in your portfolio.

In selecting marketable securities, consider the type, marketability, maturity date, rate of return, transaction cost, default risk, maximum amount to be invested, maximum/minimum dollar amount to be traded, and trend in interest rates. You have to balance the return you want against the risk you are willing to assume. As a general rule, the return on marketable securities is low, but they are liquid and safe. Risk takes the form of a lack of marketability, possible loss of principal (the amount invested), and susceptibility to changing interest rates (e.g., as interest rates rise, the price of fixed-income securities declines). You should demand a higher return when default risk is greater and the maturity period is longer.

39 Short-Term Borrowings

If you are contemplating obtaining cash from short-term borrowings, you have to take into account where, how much, and for what length of time to borrow. When seeking financing, ask for slightly more money than you think you will need in order to be prepared for unexpected eventualities.

Short-term financing may take many forms, including trade credit, personal savings, bank loans, leasing, commercial finance company loans, and insurance company loans. If your business is somewhat risky, collateral such as securities, a car, inventory, accounts receivable, or real estate, may be required to support the loan.

Trade credit is the best source of financing because it does not cost you anything. Suppliers and equipment manufacturers may be important, readily available financing sources because they want your business for their products. In addition, they understand your business operations. If there are cash problems, payments to suppliers can be delayed the most; however, there is a limit to how far you can stretch trade creditors without causing ill feelings and damaging your credit standing.

A cash advance may be received by using your *personal charge accounts*. The money obtained up to your credit limit can be used to buy inventory and pay employee salaries. The disadvantages of using your personal credit cards are the high financing cost, the need to meet minimum monthly payments, and the risk of exposing your personal assets in running the business.

Personal assets such as your personal bank account or your home may serve as a basis on which to obtain financing. You may also borrow using the cash surrender value of your life insurance. For example, if the cash surrender value of your life insurance is $200,000 and you borrow 90% against it, you can obtain $180,000. You will then have to make future payments of premium and interest on the loan to the insurance company. The benefits of employing your own funds are that the money is obtained quickly and conveniently and you are not giving up any ownership interest in the business. The disadvantages of using personal assets are that the money obtained is limited and you may lose your personal savings if the business fails.

Relatives and friends may lend you money. The benefits of using this source are that it is fast, convenient, and inexpensive. You typically do not have to furnish relatives with detailed financial information; however, borrowing from family may result in interference and arguments.

The bank may lend you money short-term without requiring collateral, allowing you to finance the purchase of inventory and to conduct normal daily operations; however, an intermediate-term loan (one to five years) will probably require some security. Intermediate-term loans are used to buy equipment, machinery, and store furnishings. Such loans may carry limitations on operations; for example, additional debt financing may be restricted and a specified working capital balance may have to be maintained.

Banks are very cautious about lending money to a *new* business. The bank will look to your character and the growth prospects of the business and its ability to generate sales and profitability. In most cases, the bank will not extend a loan so you can just pay off other obligations. The bank wants the funds to be used to improve your business's growth and profitability. The bank will probably insist that you put up some of your money to show good faith and confidence in your own business. It pays to have a good rapport with loan officers if you plan to seek additional financing at a later date.

There are many kinds of bank loans. You should select the one that best suits your particular needs at any given time. Types of bank loans include:

- *Passbook loans.* By using your passbook or bank account as security for a loan, you may finance at a lower interest rate. In the meantime, your deposit earns interest.
- *Secured loans.* Security is pledged in the event the loan is not repaid.
- *Unsecured loans.* This loan is backed by your general assets without any specific assets being pledged against the loan. Such loans may be obtained by small businesses with high credit standing; however, the interest rate on an unsecured loan is higher than on a secured one because of the greater risk faced by the bank since there is no collateral assigned.
- *Straight loans.* This loan is paid off in only one payment scheduled at the maturity date.
- *Term loans.* Term loans have monthly loan repayments covering principal and interest. A small business with a good reputation can obtain such a loan. There may be a collateral requirement.
- *Lines of credit.* This is a bank commitment to lend you money up to specified maximum amount depending on your needs. This arrangement is ideal for a seasonal small business to finance inventory purchases. The bank may assess a charge on the *unused* portion of the line of credit.

- *Cosigner loans.* If your credit is not good, the financial institution may stipulate that a third party must guarantee repayment in the event you default.

If a bank loan is not available, you may apply to a commercial finance company. Security is usually demanded. The interest rate charged on a commercial finance company loan is higher than that on a bank loan because their borrowers typically present greater risk.

The U.S. Small Business Administration may give a loan *after* you have been rejected by private lenders. Small business Administration loans typically are low-interest and require collateral. An SBA loan may be made either by the bank with a guarantee from the Small Business Administration or directly by the SBA itself.

Leasing is an attractive financing source if your cash balance is low because you need not come up with the huge cash outlay required to buy the item; however, in the long run, leasing is more costly than buying.

A *credit union* may lend your business money. Check with trade associations to see if funds are available.

A community development company may provide limited financing if you are opening up a local business, such as one based in a shopping center.

An industrial development corporation supported by your state may provide financing. Loans are usually given to buy fixed assets. The terms of the loan, including length, cost, and acceptable financial risk, vary by state. The local chamber of commerce can provide detailed information.

40 Receivables and Inventory Financing

You may be able to improve your business's cash flow by using receivables and inventory as collateral for loans. These assets represent important financing sources because they are significant in amount and relate to recurring business operations. You can therefore obtain a lot of money by using these major assets as security.

Receivables financing

Receivables financing is the use of short-term financing backed by receivables, under either a factoring or an *assignment arrangement*. The financing of accounts receivable is facilitated if customers are financially strong, sales returns are minimal, and title to the goods is received by the buyer at shipment. Its advantages are that it (1) avoids the need for long-term financing and (2) provides a recurring cash flow. Its major disadvantage is its high cost if the business has many small accounts. It varies with the amount of receivables. With the largest companies, the deals approach bank rates. On average, the loan interest is variable, prime rate plus 1 percent to 3 percent on the average daily loan balance; however, rates can range from 11 percent to 25 percent, depending on how risky the borrower's situation is. Borrowers should look at fees too. The standard in the industry is a loan fee, usually 1 percent, depending on the size of the line of credit, and an administrative fee of 0.1 percent to 0.5 percent monthly.

Factoring of accounts receivable

Factoring is the outright sale of accounts receivable to a third party *without recourse*; the purchaser assumes all credit and collection risks. The factor will typically advance you up to 80% of the customer balances. The proceeds you receive equal the face value of the receivables the factor accepts less the commission charge, usually 5% to 10%

above the prime interest rate. (The prime interest rate is the rate charged by banks to their most financially sound customers.) The amount the factor will advance depends upon the quality of the accounts receivable. The cost of factoring is the factor's commission for credit investigation, interest on the unpaid balance of advanced funds, and a discount from the face value of the receivables. The factor's charge depends on the volume of business you give the factor and the creditworthiness of your customers. Billing and collection are done by the factor. The advantages of factoring are that (1) you receive immediate cash, (2) overhead is reduced because credit investigation is no longer needed, (3) you can obtain advances as needed on a seasonal basis, (4) there are no loan restrictions or required account balances, and (5) you can receive financial advice. *Disadvantages* are that factoring involves (1) high cost, (2) possible negative customer reaction, and (3) possible antagonism from customers who are past due and who are subject to pressure from the factor.

For example, you have $10,000 per month in accounts receivable that a factor will buy, advancing you up to 75% of the receivables for an annual charge of 15% and a 1.0% fee on receivables purchased. The cost of this factoring arrangement is:

Factor fee [.01 x ($10,000 x 12)]	$1,200
Cost of borrowing [.15 x ($10,000 x .75)]	1,125
Total cost	$2,325

Consider factoring if:

- You have a high volume of receivables: many factors require a minimum monthly volume of $8,000-$10,000.
- Your customers are credit-worthy: expect factors to assess the financial stability of your customers to ensure they get paid.
- Your receivables are current: factors generally don't take on past-due accounts, or receivables of over 90 days.

To find a factor or to learn more, consult *The Edwards Directory of American Factors*, a reference guide available at many business libraries, or contact the International Factoring Association, a trade group that serves the factoring industry, at 1-800-563-1895 or **www.factoring.org.**

Assignment of accounts receivable

Assignment is the transfer of accounts receivable to a finance company with *recourse*; if the customer does not pay, you (as borrower) have to pay. The accounts receivable act as collateral, and new receivables substitute for receivables collected. Ownership of accounts receivable is not transferred. The finance company usually advances between 50% to 85% of the face value of the receivable in cash. You incur a service charge, interest on the advance, and any bad debt losses. Customer remissions continue to be made directly to you. Advantages of this system are (1) cash is immediately available, (2) cash advances are received on a seasonal basis, and (3) it avoids negative customer reaction. Its disadvantages are (1) its high cost, (2) the continued credit function, and (3) significant credit risks.

Inventory financing

Inventory financing is the use of inventory as collateral for a loan. This step usually occurs when you have fully exhausted your borrowing capacity on receivables.

Inventory financing requires the existence of marketable, nonperishable, standardized goods with fast turnover. Inventory should preferable be stable in price and expenses associated with its sale should be minimal.

The advance on inventory financing is usually higher for readily marketable inventory. A bank will usually lend you about 50% of the market value of your merchandise at an interest rate approximately three to five points over the prime interest rate.

Some ways to finance inventory are:

1. *Floating (blanket) lien*—uses entire inventory as the creditor's security.
2. *Warehouse receipt*—provides the lender an interest in the borrower's inventory if it is stored at a public warehouse. The fixed costs of this arrangement are high. In a field warehouse arrangement, the warehouser sets up a secured area directly at your location.
3. *Trust receipt*—gives the creditor title to the goods but releases them to the borrower to sell on the creditor's behalf. As goods are sold, the borrower pays the lender.
4. *Collateral certificate*—may be issued by a third party to the lender; guarantees the existence of pledged inventory.

Disadvantages of inventory financing include its high interest rate and the restrictions generally placed on the inventory.

For example, you want to finance $250,000 of inventory. Funds are needed for two months. A warehouse receipt loan may be taken out at 14% with an 80% advance against the inventory's value. The warehousing cost is $2,000 for the two-month period.

The cost of financing the inventory is:

Interest [.14 x .80 x $250,000 x (2/12)]	$4,667
Warehousing cost	2,000
Total cost	$6,667

MODULE 10

Loan Qualifications and Banking Relationships

41 Five Cs of Credit

There is a standard series of criteria lenders use to screen potential borrowers. The five elements of credit are:

1. Character (willingness to pay)
2. Capacity (cash flow)
3. Capital (wealth)
4. Collateral (security)
5. Conditions (economic environment)

- *Character* is a customer's integrity and reliability in meeting financial obligations. The borrower's credit history indicates how reliable the borrower is in paying bills on time.
- *Capacity* looks at a borrower's earning power and cash flow. Does the borrower have the ability to repay the loan out of the earnings and cash flow generated from the business?
- *Capital* analyzes a borrower's balance sheet (assets and liabilities) to reveal whether net worth is positive or negative. How much equity is there? Is the borrower's net worth adequate to meet obligations?
- *Collateral* refers to assets that can be secured and liquidated by the lender if a loan is not repaid. Which tangible assets can be used to secure a loan? Such assets may include building, office equipment, and automobile.
- Finally, *conditions* include economic factors at the time of the loan and a borrower's vulnerability to a business downturn or credit crunch. When money is available, especially at low interest rates, it is much easier to obtain credit, whereas in a credit crunch, many applicants who would normally have been approved for credit are rejected. Is the timing right for a loan application?

Once the five Cs are analyzed, a borrower is assigned to a credit rating category that reflects the perceived risk to the lender. Generally, the greater the credit risks the higher the interest rate on the loan. If risk is excessive, a borrower may be unable to obtain bank financing.

In addition, the lender may place strict restrictions on the borrower. Examples are the maintenance of a minimum cash balance and a minimum current ratio (current assets/current liabilities).

The inability to adequately finance the business will result in less growth, lower profitability, and in extreme cases, bankruptcy.

42 Bankers' Lending Criteria

Different bankers play different tunes (depending, in part, on their local market and the capital position of their institutions), but here are some of the criteria lenders generally use:

1. *Healthy cash flow.* Prudent lenders have always looked first to the cash flow of the small business as the way the loan will be repaid. The collateral-a warehouse or a house-is never viewed as the way the loan would be liquidated; it is the exit of last resort. The exception is in boom times, when collateral convinces bankers to overlook concerns about the underlying business.

   Don't forget that in bad times collateral doesn't mean very much. In fact it is a headache to lenders, since they have to get rid of the collateral fast. Therefore, when money is tight lenders want to know more about how a borrower's small business works than ever; its customers, how it competes, why it needs the cash, how it will pay back the loan. Lenders examine projections more skeptically, in some cases actually calling customers to verify its assumptions and expectations. Customer information also confirms what you have told the banker about other matters.

2. *Operational influences.* Lenders may want to have some say in how you run your operations. They may want regular updates on how the business is performing. Lenders increasingly want to have input in decisions about inventory levels and/or how many people you employ. These decisions used to be made solely by the owner.

Lenders may want more information such as financial data on debt-to-net-worth and inventory turnover (how many times inventory is sold during the year). Banks even like to put in legally binding loan covenants. For example, a loan covenant might call for a debt-to-capital ratio of 3:1, a 1.5% before-tax profit margin (net income to sales), and restrictions on capital spending and the owner's salary. Any changes to the terms need prior approval of the bank. If things slide far enough, the loan will likely be called.

3. *Lending against inventory and receivables.* No financing is more critical for many small businesses than the loans they get against inventory and receivables. But increasingly, bankers are getting uneasy about the quality of the assets behind these loans. Do they *really* want to encourage customers to buy inventory that may not sell for months or to perform services for people who won't be able to pay? No. Thus, bankers are becoming a lot more cautious. Besides doing more physical inspections of small businesses, bankers are revising their lending formulas.
4. *Cash from owners.* One way bankers downsize their risk is by demanding that owners put more capital in the business. It is not just those looking for new loans who are being asked to invest more capital; additional capital may be a requirement to *keep* the loans you have. Many lenders don't care how you do it-whether you get a new partner who brings equity into the small business or whether you put up your own money. What matters is that someone (besides the bank) is on the hook. In fact, many lenders put pressure on small business owners to guarantee debt *personally* so if you go out of business, the bank can attach your personal property (e.g., home, car) to pay off the business loan. The best-perhaps only-way to avoid guarantees is to commit more money.

43 Your Relationship with the Banker

Regardless of economic conditions or trouble in the banking sector, bankers want to lend money. They've got to! In fact, making loans is how they earn their paychecks. Your job is to package your business in such a way that your banker has confidence in you.

1. *Cut your debt.* Debt is potentially dangerous when business falls off. Lenders want to see some liquidity. No banker wants to think that he or she is absorbing the entire risk when your market begins to drag. The use of too much "other people's money" (OPM) is not welcome. You've got to reduce your dependence on bank debt, to pay down that credit line (if you have one), and build your own financial cushion.

   Costs may be cut by getting rid of weak demand or marginal products. You can speed collections by requiring customers to pay cash on delivery (COD) or by offering cash discounts for prompt payment. You should also leave cash in the business. By taking these steps, you may not eliminate your need for borrowing but you will show your banker you share his or her concerns. This will not hurt when the lender has to choose between your business and someone else's.

2. *Set the distance between you and the crowd.* Bankers think in terms of categories: if you are a food store, you will be compared with every food store the lender knows. At their fingertips, moreover, are volumes of industry data supplied by trade associations. Obviously, you cannot stop them from flipping through these books and making comparisons; however, you can attempt to correct their biases by showing them how your store really operates and how you differ from competitors.

In the past, lenders required basic information for credit decisions-two or three years' of income statements and projections for the coming year. Assuming that you were making money (and that there was sufficient collateral), all you had to prove was that you could handle the increased debt.

Today, lenders insist on more. They want to understand the details of how borrowers plan to use the money. To the extent that they are relying on cash flow more than before, they want to know as much as possible about the *quality* of that cash flow.

- Who are the customers?
- Historically, how fast have lenders been paid?
- What are the seasonal patterns in the business?
- How will you cover the time gaps between your collections and payables?

3. *Befriend your banker.* Bankers hate having bad news sprung on them. A lack of candor can jinx a relationship with your lender faster than anything. You should be friendly and close with your banker. A strong relationship will help you obtain financing when times are bad. Many lenders like to see financial updates on a quarterly and/or monthly basis, paying particular attention to significant events. If a major order falls through or you experience a strike or boycott, a diligent banker will want to hear about it (why it happened, what it means to your operation, how you intend to adjust the business). Of course, feeding bankers regular information is time-consuming when you have a business to run; however, it is part of building credibility and trust.

   In selecting a bank, consider the following:

   - Overdraft protection (allowing you to write checks for more than you have in the checking account)
   - Interest earned on deposited funds
   - Hours of operation, e.g., late hours
   - Interest and finance charges
   - Borrowing arrangements
   - Compensating balance requirements (interest-free deposit left with the bank as collateral for a loan)
   - Commitment fees for the unused portion on a line of credit
   - Availability of value-added processing (in which the bank receives your mail, opens the envelope, and prepares the check for deposit, acting as your *processing agent)*

44 Drafts, Zero-Balance Accounts (ZBAs), and Controlled Disbursement Account

Delay making payments by using *drafts*. A draft is not payable on demand but is instead presented for collection to the bank, which then asks for your approval before paying it. If you decide to accept the draft, you then deposit money with the bank to cover it. This allows you to keep a smaller average checking balance. Drafts may involve bank charges (e.g., fixed monthly fee) and the inconvenience of requiring formal approval before payment. A draft may be used to give you time to inspect merchandise received from suppliers or to assure yourself that all of the terms of sale have been fulfilled.

Assume, for example, that you pay a claim by draft of June 10 that is not deposited by the recipient at his or her local bank until June 17. The local bank sends the draft to your bank on June 19. You have until 3p.m. on June 19 to inspect and approve the draft for payment. The disbursement of cash has been delayed nine days.

Zero balance accounts (ZBAs) are special checking accounts that contain no cash balance, such as accounts for different types of disbursements including payroll and petty cash. Most commercial banks offer ZBA services, allowing you to write checks as usual; however, when the checks clear your bank against the ZBA account, the bank's computer system automatically offsets these checks (debits) with a credit from another account that you must maintain at that same bank, called a "master" ZBA account. A zero balance is held in all accounts except for the master account until payments are made.

ZBAs offer the following benefits:

- They extend disbursement float, thereby increasing the available cash pool. For example, you can put funds into your payroll and payables checking accounts only when you expect checks to clear.
- They eliminate the possibility of having excess balances in multiple accounts.
- The drawbacks to using ZBAs are:
- Banks charge for this service.
- There is overdraft potential. You must keep enough money in the master account to cover all ZBA disbursements. Without a prior arrangement such as a credit line, the bank can bounce your checks. Hence, ZBA is an aggressive strategy.

ZBAs are most effective when they are used in conjunction with an automated investment program in which funds are transferred to cover the checks clearing your checking account. The balance remaining in the ZBA is invested for a return.

Using a *controlled disbursement account*, almost all payments that must be made are known in the morning. The bank informs the firm of the total, and the firm transfers (usually by wire) the amount needed.

45 Getting Help from Money-Management Professionals

To help you manage your cash (both receiving it and using it), you may seek the advice of professionals. Experts in cash management can assist you as a business owner in investing, tax planning, retirement planning, banking, and obtaining credit and insurance. The fees professional advisors charge may be worth the cost.

The criteria to use in selecting a personal financial planner include credentials, compensation arrangements, past performance, timeliness in responding, and ability to communicate. Sources of personal financial planning include accounting and financial advisory firms, banks, brokerage firms, and insurance companies.

Professional financial planning organizations include the International Association for Financial Planning (IAFP) and the Institute of Certified Financial Planners (ICFP).

The following are some professional certification or designations used by personal financial planners:

- Certified public accountant (CPA)
- Certified financial planner (CFP)
- Chartered financial consultant (ChFC)
- Certified life underwriter (CLU)
- Chartered financial analyst (CFA)

Be forewarned that there are no restrictions on the use of the titles "financial planner" and "financial consultant."

The following table provides the areas of expertise and fee structure for personal financial planners.

Areas of Expertise and Fee Structure for Personal Financial Planners

	BEST SERVICES PROVIDED	COMPENSATION BASED ON
CPA	Taxes	Hourly fee
Attorney	Taxes and legal	Hourly fee
Commission Planner	Entire plan	Commission
Fee Planner	Entire plan	Hourly fee
Customer Representative*	Specialty (e.g., insurance investments)	Salary and/or commission

* Includes representatives from financial service companies, brokerage houses, and insurance firms.

The Certified Treasury Professional (CTP)

The Certified Treasury Professional (CTP), formerly The Certified Cash Manager (CCM), is an examination-based certification and is widely regarded by treasury managers as one of the leading credentials in the field. The CTP program is a professional certification program designed to measure an individual's knowledge of the fundamentals of cash/treasury management and to augment career development through continuing professional education. CTPs represent corporate, governmental and institutional professionals with broad responsibility in the treasury profession. CTP certification also enhances customer relations for bankers, cash management consultants and providers of related services.

Appendix

Table 1: Future value of $1 = T1(i, n)

Periods	4%	6%	8%	10%	12%	14%	20%
1	1.040	1.060	1.080	1.100	1.120	1.140	1.200
2	1.082	1.124	1.166	1.210	1.254	1.300	1.440
3	1.125	1.191	1.260	1.331	1.405	1.482	1.728
4	1.170	1.263	1.361	1.464	1.574	1.689	2.074
5	1.217	1.338	1.469	1.611	1.762	1.925	2.488
6	1.265	1.419	1.587	1.772	1.974	2.195	2.986
7	1.316	1.504	1.714	1.949	2.211	2.502	3.583
8	1.369	1.594	1.851	2.144	2.476	2.853	4.300
9	1.423	1.690	1.999	2.359	2.773	3.252	5.160
10	1.480	1.791	2.159	2.594	3.106	3.707	6.192
11	1.540	1.898	2.332	2.853	3.479	4.226	7.430
12	1.601	2.012	2.518	3.139	3.896	4.818	8.916
13	1.665	2.133	2.720	3.452	4.364	5.492	10.699
14	1.732	2.261	2.937	3.798	4.887	6.261	12.839
15	1.801	2.397	3.172	4.177	5.474	7.138	15.407
16	1.873	2.540	3.426	4.595	6.130	8.137	18.488
17	1.948	2.693	3.700	5.055	6.866	9.277	22.186
18	2.026	2.854	3.996	5.560	7.690	10.575	26.623
19	2.107	3.026	4.316	6.116	8.613	12.056	31.948
20	2.191	3.207	4.661	5.728	9.646	13.743	38.338
30	3.243	5.744	10.063	17.450	29.960	50.950	237.380
40	4.801	10.286	21.725	45.260	93.051	188.880	1469.800

Table 2: Future value of an annuity of $1 = T2(i,n)

Periods	4%	6%	8%	10%	12%	14%	20%
1	1.000	1.000	1.000	1.000	1.000	1.000	1.000
2	2.040	2.060	2.080	2.100	2.120	2.140	2.200
3	3.122	3.184	3.246	3.310	3.374	3.440	3.640
4	4.247	4.375	4.506	4.641	4.779	4.921	5.368
5	5.416	5.637	5.867	6.105	6.353	6.610	7.442
6	6.633	6.975	7.336	7.716	8.115	8.536	9.930
7	7.898	8.394	8.923	9.487	10.089	10.730	12.916
8	9.214	9.898	10.637	11.436	12.300	13.233	16.499
9	10.583	11.491	12.488	13.580	14.776	16.085	20.799
10	12.006	13.181	14.487	15.938	17.549	19.337	25.959
11	13.486	14.972	16.646	18.531	20.655	23.045	32.150
12	15.026	16.870	18.977	21.385	24.133	37.271	39.580
13	16.627	18.882	21.495	24.523	28.029	32.089	48.497
14	18.292	21.015	24.215	27.976	32.393	37.581	59.196
15	20.024	23.276	27.152	31.773	37.280	43.842	72.035
16	21.825	25.673	30.324	35.950	42.753	50.980	87.442
17	23.698	28.213	33.750	40.546	48.884	59.118	105.930
18	25.645	30.906	37.450	45.600	55.750	68.394	128.120
19	27.671	33.760	41.446	51.160	63.440	78.969	154.740
20	29.778	36.778	45.762	57.276	75.052	91.025	186.690
30	56.085	79.058	113.283	164.496	241.330	356.790	1181.900
40	95.026	154.762	259.057	442.597	767.090	1342.000	7343.900

*Payments (or receipts) at the *end* of each period.

Table 3: Present value of $1 = T3(i,n)

PERIODS	3%	4%	5%	6%	7%	8%	10%	12%	14%	16%	18%	20%	22%	24%	25%	26%	28%	30%	40%
1	.9709	.9615	.9524	.9434	.9346	.9259	.9091	.8929	.8772	.8621	.8475	.8333	.8197	.8065	.8000	.7937	.7813	.7692	.7143
2	.9426	.9246	.9070	.8900	.8734	.8573	.8264	.7972	.7695	.7432	.7182	.6944	.6719	.6504	.6400	.6299	.6104	.5917	.5102
3	.9151	.8890	.8638	.8396	.8163	.7938	.7513	.7118	.6750	.6407	.6086	.5787	.5507	.5245	.5120	.4999	.4768	.4552	.3644
4	.8885	.8548	.8227	.7921	.7629	.7350	.6830	.6355	.5921	.5523	.5158	.4823	.4514	.4230	.4096	.3968	.3725	.3501	.2603
5	.8626	.8219	.7835	.7473	.7130	.6806	.6209	.5674	.5194	.4761	.4371	.4019	.3700	.3411	.3277	.3149	.2910	.2693	.1859
6	.8375	.7903	.7462	.7050	.6663	.6302	.5645	.5066	.4556	.4104	.3704	.3349	.3033	.2751	.2621	.2499	.2274	.2072	.1328
7	.8131	.7599	.7107	.6651	.6227	.5835	.5132	.4523	.3996	.3538	.3139	.2791	.2486	.2218	.2097	.1983	.1776	.1594	.0949
8	.7894	.7307	.6768	.6274	.5820	.5403	.4665	.4039	.3506	.3050	.2660	.2326	.2038	.1789	.1678	.1574	.1388	.1226	.0678
9	.7664	.7026	.6446	.5919	.5439	.5002	.4241	.3606	.3075	.2630	.2255	.1938	.1670	.1443	.1342	.1249	.1084	.0943	.0484
10	.7441	.6756	.6139	.5584	.5083	.4632	.3855	.3220	.2697	.2267	.1911	.1615	.1369	.1164	.1074	.0992	.0847	.0725	.0346
11	.7224	.6496	.5847	.5268	.4751	.4289	.3505	.2875	.2366	.1954	.1619	.1346	.1122	.0938	.0859	.0787	.0662	.0558	.0247
12	.7014	.6246	.5568	.4970	.4440	.3971	.3186	.2567	.2076	.1685	.1372	.1122	.0920	.0757	.0687	.0625	.0517	.0429	.0176
13	.6810	.6006	.5303	.4688	.4150	.3677	.2897	.2292	.1821	.1452	.1163	.0935	.0754	.0610	.0550	.0496	.0404	.0330	.0126
14	.6611	.5775	.5051	.4423	.3878	.3405	.2633	.2046	.1597	.1252	.0985	.0779	.0618	.0492	.0440	.0393	.0316	.0254	.0090
15	.6419	.5553	.4810	.4173	.3624	.3152	.2394	.1827	.1401	.1079	.0835	.0649	.0507	.0397	.0352	.0312	.0247	.0195	.0064
16	.6232	.5339	.4581	.3936	.3387	.2919	.2176	.1631	.1229	.0930	.0708	.0541	.0415	.0320	.0281	.0248	.0193	.0150	.0046
17	.6050	.5134	.4363	.3714	.3166	.2703	.1978	.1456	.1078	.0802	.0600	.0451	.0340	.0258	.0225	.0197	.0150	.0116	.0033
18	.5874	.4936	.4155	.3503	.2959	.2502	.1799	.1300	.0946	.0691	.0508	.0376	.0279	.0208	.0180	.0156	.0118	.0089	.0023
19	.5703	.4746	.3957	.3305	.2765	.2317	.1635	.1161	.0829	.0596	.0431	.0313	.0229	.0168	.0144	.0124	.0092	.0068	.0017
20	.5537	.4564	.3769	.3118	.2584	.2145	.1486	.1037	.0728	.0514	.0365	.0261	.0187	.0135	.0115	.0098	.0072	.0053	.0012
21	.5375	.4388	.3589	.2942	.2415	.1987	.1351	.0926	.0638	.0443	.0309	.0217	.0154	.0109	.0092	.0078	.0056	.0040	.0009
22	.5219	.4220	.3418	.2775	.2257	.1839	.1228	.0826	.0560	.0382	.0262	.0181	.0126	.0088	.0074	.0062	.0044	.0031	.0006
23	.5067	.4057	.3256	.2618	.2109	.1703	.1117	.0738	.0491	.0329	.0222	.0151	.0103	.0071	.0059	.0049	.0034	.0024	.0004
24	.4919	.3901	.3101	.2470	.1971	.1577	.1015	.0659	.0431	.0284	.0188	.0126	.0085	.0057	.0047	.0039	.0027	.0018	.0003
25	.4776	.3751	.2953	.2330	.1842	.1460	.0923	.0588	.0378	.0245	.0160	.0105	.0069	.0046	.0038	.0031	.0021	.0014	.0002
26	.4637	.3607	.2812	.2198	.1722	.1352	.0839	.0525	.0331	.0211	.0135	.0087	.0057	.0037	.0030	.0025	.0016	.0011	.0002
27	.4502	.3468	.2678	.2074	.1609	.1252	.0763	.0469	.0291	.0182	.0115	.0073	.0047	.0030	.0024	.0019	.0013	.0008	.0001
28	.4371	.3335	.2551	.1956	.1504	.1159	.0693	.0419	.0255	.0157	.0097	.0061	.0038	.0024	.0019	.0015	.0010	.0006	.0001
29	.4243	.3207	.2429	.1846	.1406	.1073	.0630	.0374	.0224	.0135	.0082	.0051	.0031	.0020	.0015	.0012	.0008	.0005	.0001
30	.4120	.3083	.2314	.1741	.1314	.0994	.0573	.0334	.0196	.0116	.0070	.0042	.0026	.0016	.0012	.0010	.0006	.0004	.0000
40	.3066	.2083	.1420	.0972	.0668	.0460	.0221	.0107	.0053	.0026	.0013	.0007	.0004	.0002	.0001	.0001	.0001	.0000	.0000

Table 4: Present value of an annuity of $1 = T4(i,n)

Periods	3%	4%	5%	6%	7%	8%	10%	12%	14%	16%	18%	20%	22%	24%
1	.9709	.9615	.9524	.9434	.9346	.9259	.9091	.8929	.8772	.8621	.8475	.8333	.8197	.8065
2	1.9135	1.8861	1.8594	1.8334	1.8080	1.7833	1.7355	1.6901	1.6467	1.6052	1.5656	1.5278	1.4915	1.4568
3	2.8286	2.7751	2.7232	2.6730	2.6243	2.5771	2.4869	2.4018	2.3216	2.2459	2.1743	2.1065	2.0422	1.9813
4	3.7171	3.6299	3.5460	3.4651	3.3872	3.3121	3.1699	3.0373	2.9137	2.7982	2.6901	2.5887	2.4936	2.4043
5	4.5797	4.4518	4.3295	4.2124	4.1002	3.9927	3.7908	3.6048	3.4331	3.2743	3.1272	2.9906	2.8636	2.7454
6	5.4172	5.2421	5.0757	4.9173	4.7665	4.6229	4.3553	4.1114	3.8887	3.6847	3.4976	3.3255	3.1669	3.0205
7	6.2303	6.0021	5.7864	5.5824	5.3893	5.2064	4.8684	4.5638	4.2883	4.0386	3.8115	3.6046	3.4155	3.2423
8	7.0197	6.7327	6.4632	6.2098	5.9713	5.7466	5.3349	4.9676	4.6389	4.3436	4.0776	3.8372	3.6193	3.4212
9	7.7861	7.4353	7.1078	6.8017	6.5152	6.2469	5.7590	5.3282	4.9464	4.6065	4.3030	4.0310	3.7863	3.5655
10	8.5302	8.1109	7.7217	7.3601	7.0236	6.7101	6.1446	5.6502	5.2161	4.8332	4.4941	4.1925	3.9232	3.6819
11	9.2526	8.7605	8.3064	7.8869	7.4987	7.1390	6.4951	5.9377	5.4527	5.0286	4.6560	4.3271	4.0354	3.7757
12	9.9540	9.3851	8.8633	8.3838	7.9427	7.5361	6.8137	6.1944	5.6603	5.1971	4.7932	4.4392	4.1274	3.8514
13	10.6350	9.9856	9.3936	8.8527	8.3577	7.9038	7.1034	6.4235	5.8424	5.3423	4.9095	4.5327	4.2028	3.9124
14	11.2961	10.5631	9.8986	9.2950	8.7455	8.2442	7.3667	6.6282	6.0021	5.4675	5.0081	4.6106	4.2646	3.9616
15	11.9379	11.1184	10.3797	9.7122	9.1079	8.5595	7.6061	6.8109	6.1422	5.5755	5.0916	4.6755	4.3152	4.0013
16	12.5611	11.6523	10.8378	10.1059	9.4466	8.8514	7.8237	6.9740	6.2651	5.6685	5.1624	4.7296	4.3567	4.0333
17	13.1661	12.1657	11.2741	10.4773	9.7632	9.1216	8.0216	7.1196	6.3729	5.7487	5.2223	4.7746	4.3908	4.0591
18	13.7535	12.6593	11.6896	10.8276	10.0591	9.3719	8.2014	7.2497	6.4674	5.8178	5.2732	4.8122	4.4187	4.0799
19	14.3238	13.1339	12.0853	11.1581	10.3356	9.6036	8.3649	7.3658	6.5504	5.8775	5.3162	4.8435	4.4415	4.0967
20	14.8775	13.5903	12.4622	11.4699	10.5940	9.8181	8.5136	7.4694	6.6231	5.9288	5.3527	4.8696	4.4603	4.1103
21	15.4150	14.0292	12.8212	11.7641	10.8355	10.0168	8.6487	7.5620	6.6870	5.9731	5.3837	4.8913	4.4756	4.1212
22	15.9369	14.4511	13.1630	12.0416	11.0612	10.2007	8.7715	7.6446	6.7429	6.0113	5.4099	4.9094	4.4882	4.1300
23	16.4436	14.8568	13.4886	12.3034	11.2722	10.3711	8.8832	7.7184	6.7921	6.0442	5.4321	4.9245	4.4985	4.1371
24	16.9355	15.2470	13.7986	12.5504	11.4693	10.5288	8.9847	7.7843	6.8351	6.0726	5.4509	4.9371	4.5070	4.1428
25	17.4131	15.6221	14.0939	12.7834	11.6536	10.6748	9.0770	7.8431	6.8729	6.0971	5.4669	4.9476	4.5139	4.1474
26	17.8768	15.9828	14.3752	13.0032	11.8258	10.8100	9.1609	7.8957	6.9061	6.1182	5.4804	4.9563	4.5196	4.1511
27	18.3270	16.3296	14.6430	13.2105	11.9867	10.9352	9.2372	7.9426	6.9352	6.1364	5.4919	4.9636	4.5243	4.1542
28	18.7641	16.6631	14.8981	13.4062	12.1371	11.0511	9.3066	7.9844	6.9607	6.1520	5.5016	4.9697	4.5281	4.1566
29	19.1885	16.9837	15.1411	13.5907	12.2777	11.1584	9.3696	8.0218	6.9830	6.1656	5.5098	4.9747	4.5312	4.1585
30	19.6004	17.2920	15.3725	13.7648	12.4090	11.2578	9.4269	8.0552	7.0027	6.1772	5.5168	4.9789	4.5338	4.1601
40	23.1148	19.7928	17.1591	15.0463	13.3317	11.9246	9.7791	8.2438	7.1050	6.2335	5.5482	4.9966	4.5439	4.1659

Questions and Answers

1. What are the major sources of cash?

There are two major categories of cash inflows: operating and nonoperating. Operating cash inflows are derived from the major activities of the small business. They come from the sale of merchandise or the performance of services. Examples are cash sales and collections from customers. Nonoperating cash inflows are derived from incidental transactions such as royalties, rental income, dividend income, interest income, sale of marketable securities, and borrowings.

2. What are the factors that affect cash collections from sales?

It is necessary to identify the factors affecting the ultimate realization of cash because that offers a base from which to develop a cash forecast. Ask the following questions: 1. What is total sales volume or dollars? 2. What amount represents cash sales? 3. What amount of receivables are collectible? 4. What are the reasons for uncollectible accounts? 5. How much are expected sales returns and allowances?

3. What are the major uses of cash?

There are two major categories of cash outflows: operating and nonoperating. Operating cash outflows are typically the regular disbursements such as payroll, inventory purchase, rent, and insurance. Nonoperating cash outflows originate from capital expenditures, dividend payments, interest, loan repayments, tax payments, purchase of marketable securities, and redemption of securities.

4. What is a "golden rule" in cash management?

A useful guide is to speed up collections and stretch out payments as long as practically possible.

5. Can you keep your cash balance at zero or near zero?

It is not going to be easy; however, at least in theory, it is possible under two conditions: (1) a perfect forecast of net cash flows (cash inflows *minus* cash outflows) over the planning horizon and (2) perfect matching of cash receipts and disbursements. Unfortunately, these two conditions are not easily realized in reality. Perfect cash forecasting is not possible; inflows and outflows are not exactly timed the same. Some inflows and outflows are uncertain. Some cash inflows and cash outflows are irregular; others are more continual.

6. How do you deal with a banker?

Here are some strategies for dealing with a banker. 1. Never ask a banker for money. Act as though you do not need any money; ask for advice and information. 2. Lure a banker to your turf. On your own turf, you will feel more at ease and be in a stronger position. Say "Why not come out for look-see? We could have lunch." 3. While negotiating with one bank, get yourself a backup banker. Shop around. 4. Once you have obtained your loan or line of credit, stay in touch with your banker. Keep you banker friend informed about your business.

7. What are the types of questions you should ask prospective bankers?

Here are some typical questions to ask. What are your lending limits? What are your views on small businesses like mine? What experience do you have in working with my line of business? Do you make Small Business Administration-guaranteed loans? What are your criteria for loan decisions? Would you describe the loan approval process? How long will it take for the loan to be approved? What do you think of my business plan?

8. In what types of investments do small businesses maintain excess idle cash?

1. Income-producing investment accounts until one can find better use for the money. For example, a small business may invest in money-market funds until the money is required to purchase materials, pay overhead, or meet debt payments.

2. Investments by financial service or investment companies. These firms invest in money market instruments because their return is greater than their cost of funds. For example, a bank borrows funds in the form of certificates of deposit at a cost of 6% and invests the funds in mortgages at 11%, and makes a profit of 5% minus operating expenses.

9. What are the types of money market investments?

Money market investments are short-term debt securities maturing in less than 90 days. The small business owner must have a right mix of these funds in terms of maturity so the money may be available to pay the company's bills on time. Typically, the categories of money market investments include the following:

1. Savings accounts, 2. Money market deposit accounts (MMDA), 3. Certificates of deposit (CDs), 4. Commercial paper, 5. Repurchase agreements (Repos).

10. What are the keys to good banking relationships?

There are four important factors associated with a healthy banking relationship. 1. Understand your responsibility, what is expected of the business and how certain transactions will be viewed. 2. Provide the bank with pertinent information about your business and how it is progressing. 3. Define and agree on the terms of the banking relationship, commitments by each party, and a targeted compensation to the bank for its services. 4. Communicate as often as possible. An effective communication channel will accommodate exceptions, problems, or changes of plans.

11. What is the right bank for you?

In selecting the right bank for your business you should review closely the services, relationships, and the financial strength of each prospective bank. This review should include deposit services, credit needs, investment services, banking advice, and location. Services offered and quality of services vary from bank to bank. In addition to services provided, industry expertise, compensation requirements, and personal relationships are important considerations when selecting a bank.

12. Can a computer help in cash management?

There is no doubt about it. Computer spreadsheet software such as Excel can help set up a cash budget and perform "what-if" analysis. There are popular cash flow software including *Cash Pass* and *Up Your Cash Flow* Software.

Glossary

Advance

1. Money given to an employee before it is earned, such as an advance against salary.
2. Payment received from customers in advance for work, goods, or services.
3. Money given by a banker to a borrower in advance usually short-term, and in the form of an overdraft.

After-tax cash flow net cash flow (cash revenue less cash expenses) after taxes have been subtracted. It is the cash flow generated from operations.

Bank reconciliation the process of reconciling the differences between the bank statement and the checkbook balance. The checkbook balance must be the same as the bank balance at the end of the period after accounting for (1) items shown on the checkbook but not on the bank statement (e.g., outstanding checks) and (2) items shown on the bank statement but not on the checkbook (e.g.. bank service charges).

Banker's acceptance time draft drawn by a business firm whose payment is guaranteed by the bank's "acceptance" of it. It is especially important in foreign trade, because it allows the seller of goods to be certain that the buyer's draft will actually have funds behind it.

Bankruptcy the inability to pay debts when due. A business is insolvent in a legal sense when its financial condition is such that total liabilities exceed the fair market value of the assets.

Billing cycle the time period between periodic billings for merchandise or services rendered, typically one month.

Bounced check a check that has been returned for insufficient funds.

Bridge loan short-term loan that is made in expectation of intermediate- or long-term loans. The interest rate on a bridge loan is generally higher than that on longer-term loans. An example is a temporary loan made to permit a closing on a building purchase prior to a closing on long-term mortgage financing.

Cash and carry a requirement that a customer pay a retail store in cash for a good or service and either take immediate delivery or arrange for delivery (at a charge).

Cash before delivery a requirement by a seller that the buyer pay for goods before delivery. A discount may be given for immediate payment. The seller may do this when the buyer's ability to pay is questionable.

Cash budget a budget for cash planning and control that presents anticipated cash inflow and cash outflow for a specified time period. The cash budget helps the owner keep cash balances in reasonable relationship to needs. It assists in avoiding idle cash and possible cash shortages. The cash budget shows beginning cash, cash receipts, cash payments, and ending cash.

Cash disbursement (payments) journal book used to record all payments made in cash such as for accounts payable, merchandise purchases, and operating expenses.

Cash equivalent

1. Immediately realizable money that can be obtained in exchange of goods or services.
2. Financial instruments of high liquidity and safety (e.g.. Treasury bill, money-market fund).

Cash flow

1. Cash receipts minus cash disbursements from a given operation or asset for a given period.
2. Cash basis net income.

Cash flow statement statement showing from what sources cash has come into the business and on what the cash has been spent. Cash flow is broken down into operating, investing, and financing activities.

Cash receipts journal book used to record all transactions involving the receipt of cash. Examples are cash sales, receipt of interest and dividend income, collections from customer accounts, and cash sale of assets. Typically, there are separate columns for the date, explanation, cash debit, sales discount debit, other debit, account credit, accounts receivable credit, and other credit.

Cash shortage and overage situation in which the physical amount of cash on hand differs from the book recorded amount of cash. This is a particular problem with over-the-counter cash receipts.

Certificate of deposit (CD) special type of time deposit. *A* CD is an investment instrument, available at financial institutions, that generally offers a fixed rate of return for a specified period. The depositor agrees not to withdraw funds until the CD matures.

If the funds are withdrawn, a significant penalty is charged. The fixed rate of return normally increases with the amount or the term of the investment.

Certified check depositor's check that a bank guarantees to pay. The funds are precommitted.

Collection period number of days it takes to collect accounts receivable. The collection period can be compared to the terms of sale.

Commercial paper short-term unsecured note issued by financially strong businesses.

Compensating balance the balance a borrower must maintain on deposit in a bank account, representing a given percentage of the loan. No interest is earned on this balance which increases the effective interest rate on the loan.

Concentration banking acceleration of cash collections from customers by having funds sent to several regional banks and transferred to a *main* concentration account in another hank. The transfer of funds can be accomplished electronically.

Credit a loan extended to a business or individual and payable at a later date.

Credit analysis process of evaluating, before a line of credit is extended, whether a credit applicant meets the firm's credit standards.

Credit application a form used to record information regarding a credit applicant's ability to repay the debt.

Credit bureau an agency' that gathers credit information about customers.

Credit limit **a** specified amount beyond which a credit customer may not buy on credit.

Credit line specified amount of money available to a borrower from a bank, usually for one year. A credit line is a moral, not a contractual, commitment, and no commitment fee is charged.

Credit memorandum a form issued by a seller to a buyer indicating that the seller is reducing the amount the buyer owes.

Credit rating **a** rating to help the business determine if a credit applicant should be granted credit. It is based on factors such as the applicant's job history, income, assets owned, and credit history.

Credit receipt written evidence of merchandise returned and the selling price.

Creditor business or individual that has extended credit and is owed money.

Debit memorandum a form issued by a seller to a buyer indicating that the seller is increasing the amount the buyer owes.

Default failure to meet the conditions of a loan contract. It generally refers to the failure to meet interest and/or principal payments.

Demand deposit deposit from which funds may be drawn on demand and from which funds may be transferred to another party by means of a check.

Direct deposit of payroll an agreement to utilize an automated clearing house to deposit worker paychecks automatically into employee accounts.

Discharge of bankruptcy an order in which the bankrupt debtor is relieved of responsibility to pay his or her obligations.

Discount loan **a** loan in which the whole interest charge is deducted in advance from the face value of a loan, reducing the proceeds received. This increases the effective interest cost of the loan.

Dunning letter notices that insistently demand repayment of debts from customers.

Electronic funds transfer paperless funds transfer.

Equal Credit Opportunity Act a **US** federal law making it illegal to discriminate when giving credit.

Fee compensation the payment to the bank to compensate it for services rendered.

Float

1. Amount of funds represented by checks that have been issued but not yet collected.
2. Time between the deposit of checks in a bank and payment. Due to the time difference, many firms are able to "play the float," that is, to write checks against money not presently in the firm's bank account.

Illiquid

1. Lacking enough liquid assets, such as cash and marketable securities, to cover short-term obligations.
2. Having current liabilities exceed current assets.

Impaired credit **a** reduction in credit given by a business to a customer who has experienced deterioration in creditworthiness.

Insolvency failure of a company to meet its obligations as they become due. An analysis of insolvency concentrates on the operating and capital structure of the business. The proportion of long-term debt in the capital structure must also be considered.

Installment credit a type of consumer credit in which the consumer pays the amount in equal payments, usually monthly.

Installment loan a loan that is repaid in a series of periodic, fixed scheduled payments instead of in a lump sum.

Installment sale a sale in which periodic cash payments will be received over time.

Inventory turnover the number of times inventory is sold during the year. it equals cost of goods sold divided by the average dollar balance. Average inventory equals the beginning and ending balances divided by two.

Line of credit the maximum preapproved amount that a business may borrow.

Liquid the state of having sufficient cash and near-cash assets to meet current debt.

Liquid asset cash asset (e.g., cash or an unrestricted bank account) or readily marketable security. A liquid asset can be converted into cash in a short time without a material concession in price. Excluded from this definition are accounts receivable and inventory.

Liquidation process of closing a business entity, including selling or disposing of the assets, paying the liabilities, and having whatever is left over returned to the owners.

Lockbox box in a U.S. Postal Service facility, used to facilitate collection of customer remittances. The use of a lockbox reduces processing float. The recipient's local bank collects from these boxes periodically during the day and deposits the funds in the appropriate corporate account.

Marketable security readily tradable equity or debt security with quoted prices.

Master account account from which funds are transferred to zero balance accounts when needed.

Money

1. Cash.
2. Term broadly used to refer to a medium of exchange and unit of value.

Money market market for short-term (less than one year) debt securities. Examples of money-market securities include U.S. Treasury bills and commercial paper.

Money order check issued by a bank to a payee when an individual gives the bank funds in exchange. Payees sometimes require a money order since it is, in effect, guaranteed payment.

Mutual fund portfolio of securities professionally managed by the sponsoring management company or investment company that issues shares to investors.

Negative cash flow a situation in which cash inflows are less than cash outflows. This is an unfavorable situation that may result in liquidity problems.

Not-sufficient-funds check (NSF check) check not covered by sufficient bank balance. In preparing its bank reconciliation the depositing entity must deduct the NSF check from the cash book balance.

Operating cycle average time period between buying inventory and receiving cash proceeds from its eventual sale. It is determined by adding the number of days inventory is held and the collection period for accounts receivable.

Out-of-pocket cost actual cash outlays made during the period for payroll, advertising, and other operating expenses. Depreciation is not an out-of-pocket cost since it involves no current cash expenditure.

Overdraft

1. Negative balance in a checking account caused by payment of checks drawn against insufficient funds.
2. Situation where a borrower draws money against a previously established line of credit. The basic cost to the borrower is the interest rate levied on the daily overdraft balance.

Payment plan **a** plan specifying the dates and amounts of payments to he made under a financing agreement.

Petty cash fund minimal amount of money kept on hand by a business entity to meet small expenditures (e.g., postage. taxi fare).

Portfolio **a** group of securities held in order to reduce risk by diversification.

Prime rate interest rate charged by banks to their most financially sound customers.

Quick asset current asset that can be converted into cash in a short time. Examples are cash, marketable securities, and accounts receivable. Certain current assets, such as inventory and prepaid expenses, are excluded.

Retail lockbox a lockbox that collects numerous small-dollar remittances from consumers.

Secured loan a loan requiring certain assets to be pledged as collateral.

Stop payment instruction to the bank not to honor a check when presented. As long as the check has not been cashed, the maker has up to six months to present a stop payment notice; however, a stop payment right does not apply' to electronic funds transfers.

Sweep account a bank account in which excess funds are automatically transferred into an interest-earning account at the same bank.

Target balance average collected balance to be maintained at the bank to compensate it for services provided to the small business.

Temporary investments strategy of using seasonal excess of cash to invest in marketable securities that the company intends to convert back into cash within one year. The investments produce dividend and/or interest income as well as possible capital appreciation for the company.

Term loan immediate- to long-term secured loan granted to a business by a commercial bank, insurance company, or commercial finance company, usually to finance capital equipment or provide working capital. The loan is amortized over a fixed period.

Tight money a situation in which fewer funds are made available to borrowers by lending institutions and creditors. If available, the loans carry higher interest rates.

Time deposit savings account at a financial institution that earns interest hut is not legally subject to withdrawal on demand or transfer by check. The depositor can withdraw only by giving notice.

Time value of money value of money at different time periods. As a rule, one dollar today is worth more than one dollar tomorrow. The time value of money is a critical consideration in financial decisions.

Treasury bill short-term obligation of the federal government, commonly called a T-bill. Treasury bills carry no coupon but are sold on a discount basis. Denominations range from $10,000 to $1 million. The yields on T-bills are lower than those on any other marketable securities due to their virtually risk-free nature.

Truth-in-Lending Act a federal law protecting credit purchases. The most important provision is the requirement that both the dollar amount of finance charges and the annual percentage rate charged be disclosed.

Unbundling an approach in which the business only pays for bank services actually used.

Unsecured loan a loan on which no collateral is required.

Index